I CAN'T WAIT!

52 STORIES OF KIDS
WHO CHANGED THEIR WORLD...THAT YOU CAN READ TOGETHER

WRITTEN & ILLUSTRATED BY
TIM ELMORE

Copyright © 2023 by Tim Elmore.

All rights reserved.

All rights reserved. No portion of this book may be reproduced, stored in a retrieval system, or transmitted in any form or by any means-electronic, mechanical, photocopy, recording, or other except for brief quotations in printed reviews, without prior permission from the publisher.

Published in Atlanta, Georgia, by Maxwell Leadership Publishing in association with Growing Leaders, Inc. www.GrowingLeaders.com

ISBN: 978-1-7369001-3-0
Printed in the United States of America

Library of Congress Cataloguing-in-Publication Datacation Data

Table of Contents

How to Get the Most out of This Book vi

52 Stories of Kids Who Influenced Their World

1. Virgil vs. the Hurricane (Virgil Smith) 2
2. Let There Be Light! (Ann Makosinski) 6
3. Turning an Interruption Into an Introduction (Isaac Newton) 10
4. The Unlikely Leader (Greta Thunberg) 14
5. A Different Kind of Homework (Trevor Ferrell) 18
6. Courage Creates Commitment (Joan of Arc) 22
7. The Socks that Talk (Jim Henson) 26
8. Turning Tragedy into Triumph (Malala Yousafzai) 30
9. Never Too Young (Ayush Kumar) 34
10. Lucy's Love Blankets (Lucy Blaylock) 38
11. It All Starts with an Idea (Marsai Martin) 42
12. Inventing Eva (Julio Rios Cantu) 46
13. Earning an "A" (Robert Heft) 50
14. Turning Trash into Treasure (Kelvin Doe) 54
15. When Your Problem Becomes Your Purpose (Louis Braille) 58
16. Hungry to Help the Hungry (Sagen Woolrey) 62
17. Not Too Young to Lead (De'Monte Love) 66
18. Tough Times Made Her Tough (Sonia Sotomayor) 70
19. She Has a Way with Words (Oprah Winfrey) 74
20. The Sandless Sandbag (Peyton Robertson) 78
21. Find a Need and Fill It (Jim Casey) 82
22. When Her Talent Met a Problem (Dasia Taylor) 86
23. The Power of a Name (Beau Jessup) 90
24. Getting the Story Straight (Avi Schiffmann) 94
25. Born to Perform (Simone Biles) 98
26. A Mountaintop Experience (The Kids Who Climbed Mount Everest) 102
27. The Shoe That Grows (Kenton Lee) 106

28. Respond, Don't React (Six Teens in Nashville) 110
29. What We Nourish Will Flourish (Shamma Al Mazrui) 114
30. I Have a Dream (Michael "Martin Luther" King) 118
31. There's an App for That (Vinay Kumar) 122
32. Balance Your Talents (Tiger Woods) 126
33. A Little Saint (Mary Teresa Bojaxhiu) 130
34. The Music Was in Him (Wolfgang Amadeus Mozart) 134
35. Freedom Isn't Free (Girls of Iran) 138
36. Turning a Bad Day Around (Liam Elkind) 142
37. Getting Caught by the Police (Norris Guidry) 146
38. Finding Planets While Stargazing (Michelle Kunimoto) 150
39. No One Eats Alone (Denis Estimon) 154
40. Amy's Big Decision (Amy Waldroop) 158
41. When Homework Pays Off (Evan Spiegel) 162
42. Learning to Teach Yourself (Albert Einstein) 166
43. Students Helping Students (Karly Hou) 170
44. How Do You Like Them Apples? (Steve Jobs) 174
45. A Small Step that Made a Big Difference (Tammy Hendley) 178
46. Screenager (Mark Zuckerberg) 182
47. Vision for the Blind (Shubham Banerjee) 186
48. Use What You Have (Stephen Spielberg) 190
49. Mo's Bows (Mo Bridges) 194
50. Me and the Bees (Mikaila Ulmer) 198
51. Creative Clothes (Maya Penn) 202
52. A Light for Others (Ida Lewis) 206

Appendix

Why I've Given My Life to Developing Young Leaders 211
Why Today Is the Right Time to Develop Young Leaders 214
How to Spot a Leader Early 216
About the Author 221

How to Get the Most out of This Book

It's a cliché, but it's true—we hear a lot of bad news in the media today. Everywhere we turn, a story about a problem or a crisis pops up. Terrorism. Job losses. Mental health issues. Mass shootings. Economic downturns that force people to lose jobs. It can get a little discouraging.

This book is full of stories that represent good news. They're about young people under 25 years old who did something unusual. Their stories are amazing conversation starters for kids, parents, teachers, coaches, or youth leaders. These kids didn't wait until they were older to start changing their world. You might say their mantra was: "I can't wait!"

Most of them would not consider themselves to be extraordinary. I am sure most felt very ordinary. But they did something different. Some of them got started at age six, while others got their start a little later, as a young adult. Here is what's interesting about their stories:

- Some were very smart, but certainly not all of them.
- Some were very talented, but certainly not all of them.
- Some were very good-looking, but certainly not all of them.
- Some were strong-willed, but certainly not all of them.
- Some were great speakers, but certainly not all of them.
- Some were physically strong, but certainly not all of them.

In this book, you will read stories of young people from various races and backgrounds and languages and ages who decided to start changing their world right now, instead of assuming they must wait until they felt ready. The stories are about young people who lived during different periods in history—some in the 1400s, while others are living today.

I believe what they all have in common is that they were uncommon. Today's generation of kids, teens, and young adults live in an amazing time. Since ours is a day of smart technology and many of us own a portable device, kids feel empowered. They know more information at a younger age than past generations of youth. They have a better chance at getting a good education than past generations of kids. They have more access to tools, insights, videos, and books than former generations did, and millions of today's young people are taking advantage of that advantage. Our world is on-demand, instant-access, and search-friendly, making it possible to solve problems and serve people better than ever before.

I believe technology is a wonderful servant, but a horrible master. What if we used it to do something helpful for others, not just entertain ourselves? What if we focused on leveraging it to solve problems and serve people? What could happen to our world?

My goal isn't to make you feel guilty for not doing more, but to make you feel inspired. I hope these stories start conversations between you and your family and friends. Each one is short, so you can read it in the morning, at dinnertime, or before you go to bed. Each has some discussion questions to spark your interaction. If you'd like to go deeper on any story, go to www.icantwaitbook.com to watch a video. I hope that these stories will inspire you to live a better story.

52 Stories of Kids Who Influenced Their World

I CAN'T WAIT!

Virgil Smith

Virgil vs. the Hurricane

Virgil was a typical middle school student who loved playing video games. One night, he was playing an online game with his friend Keshaun (who lived nearby) when heard a loud noise outside his apartment. It was a storm coming, and Virgil had no idea how dangerous it was.

The storm was Hurricane Harvey.

When water began seeping into his home around two a.m., Virgil, along with his sister and his mother, grabbed their phones and climbed to their apartment building's second floor for safety. They had hoped to wait out the storm there, protected from the hurricane. It was then that Virgil got a phone call from his friend asking for help. Keshaun and his family were trapped by rising floodwaters.

Instead of waiting for an adult to do something or even waiting for permission, Virgil quickly sprang into action. He felt it was his duty to help. It was the right thing to do.

He scampered downstairs to his apartment, grabbed an air mattress, and used it as a raft, paddling to his friend's apartment to save him and his family. Once he got them to safety, Virgil began hearing noises from other parts of his complex in Dickinson, Texas. They were the voices of neighbors crying for help. The neighborhood was flooding with water. Once again, Virgil didn't wait for an adult to do something, or to get permission from anyone.

Virgil hopped on his makeshift raft again and paddled around the neighborhood near his apartment, pulling people out of dangerous, flooded homes.

He did this for hours. When all was said and done that night, Virgil had saved seventeen lives.

There were lots of reasons why Virgil could have excused himself from this heroism:

- It was late at night and he was tired.
- He was young and inexperienced.
- He had asthma.
- The storm was one of the largest hurricanes to ever hit that area.
- He's an introvert, not an extrovert.

The soft-spoken teen, who probably still doesn't see himself as a leader, modeled brilliant leadership and hardly spoke a word about it afterward. He saw it as something he could do and felt he didn't need to wait for someone else to do it.

In the spring of 2018, Virgil Smith was awarded a Citizen Hero award from the Congressional Medal of Honor Society.

Not bad for a kid in the eighth grade.

Think It Over, Talk It Over

1. What do you admire most about Virgil's story?
2. What do you think motivated Virgil? What made him able to think he could do it?
3. Virgil took the resources he had and used them to solve a problem. Can you think of any resources you have that you could use to serve other people?

To watch a video about this young leader, go to: ICantWaitBook.com

I CAN'T WAIT!

Ann Makosinski

Let There Be Light!

When Ann was a young child, she loved science. She didn't claim to be super smart, but she was very curious about how everything worked. Her first toy was a box of transistors. She began participating in local science fairs in Canada, where she lived, when she was eleven years old.

When she was in tenth grade, Ann got inspired with her first big project.

She had a friend who lived in the Philippines, and they often interacted on Facebook. When Ann asked her how she was doing in school, her friend quietly replied, "Not good." Ann couldn't understand it because her friend was so intelligent. But her Filipino Facebook pal explained that her house had no electricity, so when the sun went down, it was too dark to study or do homework. As a result, she failed a class. Ann could hardly believe her ears. Her friend had no light to study by, so she flunked out.

Something had to be done, and Ann felt like she should be the one to do it. She wanted to solve this problem. She instantly remembered her love of science and her passion for inventions that helped people. She wrote down a few possibilities and began working on an idea for a flashlight that required no batteries for electricity.

After researching the topic and experimenting with all kinds of prospects—Ann came up with her answer: The Hollow Flashlight.

It runs off the heat of a human hand. When you hold it, your body heat—the thermoelectric effect—powers the flashlight's LED bulb. At any given moment, the heat from our bodies produces enough energy to power a hundred-watt light bulb. In one sense, we are always wasting energy that could be used. Now her friend can read or study anytime, by holding the Hollow Flashlight or by wearing a hat with the light on it. Genius!

The invention won Ann an award at the 2013 Google Science Fair, as well as numerous awards at the Intel Science and Engineering Fair. Ann's project has been covered in numerous media outlets. She appeared on The Tonight Show with Jimmy Fallon and was named one of TIME's "30 Under 30."

Ann hopes to manufacture her flashlight, bringing the invention to developing countries and including them in emergency kits. Ann also invented the eDrink: a coffee mug that harvests the excess heat of your hot drink and converts it into electricity to charge a phone. She was voted the 2016 Popular Science Young Inventor of the Year.

Think It Over, Talk It Over

1. What do you like most about Ann's story? What makes it interesting?
2. What do you think motivated Ann to invent this flashlight? What sparked her action?
3. Ann found a way to connect her interest in science with a problem to be solved. Can you think of anything you are curious about that you could use to solve a problem?

To watch a video about this young leader, go to: ICantWaitBook.com

I CAN'T WAIT!

Isaac Newton

Turning an Interruption Into an Introduction

In the spring of 2020, the entire world experienced the coronavirus pandemic and faced a quarantine. I'm often surprised by what can be achieved when people must slow down.

Did you know that Isaac Newton was a college student during the Great Plague of London in 1665? Much like COVID-19, people had enough sense to practice "social distancing." And thanks to Isaac's discipline, he turned his free time into a great time. He invested it.

And that's when the magic happened.

Cambridge University sent students home, so Newton returned to his family about sixty miles away from campus. Without his teachers to guide him, he flourished. He loved choosing what and how he wanted to study. The year he spent away was later referred to as his "year of wonders."

First of all, he continued working on a math theory that he'd developed earlier. Believe it or not, the papers he wrote became the math subject we now call calculus.

Second, he acquired some prisms and began experimenting with them in his room, even boring a hole in his shutters so a small beam of light would shine through. From his explorations emerged his theories on optics, which we still use today.

Third, outside his window was an apple tree. Yes, the apple tree we've all heard about. While parts of the narrative are urban legend, his assistant confirmed much of it is true. It was while sitting under that tree, an apple fell which launched his thinking. "The same power of gravity which made an apple fall to the ground was not limited to a certain distance from the earth (to a tree) but must extend farther than was usually thought. 'Why not as high as the moon?'" From this apple, Newton developed his theory on the law of gravity and his laws of motion.

What We Learn From Isaac Newton
Back in London, a fourth of the population would die of the plague between 1665–1666. It was one of many outbreaks during the four hundred years that the Black Plague ravaged Europe. But today, we've all benefited from it. Isaac Newton returned to Cambridge in 1667, with his theories in hand. Within six months, he was made a fellow.

Two years later, he became a professor. Not bad for a young guy. He took advantage of his time alone during a pandemic. He turned an interruption into an introduction to brand-new discoveries.

Think It Over, Talk It Over

1. What choice did Isaac make to ensure his time alone would be productive instead of wasteful?
2. Isaac didn't run from solitude and silence; he embraced them. Is this hard for you? Why?
3. Newton found a way to take "ownership" of his days in quarantine. What could you do to better take charge of your time and use it to grow personally?

To watch a video about this young leader, go to: ICantWaitBook.com

I CAN'T WAIT!

Greta Thunberg

The Unlikely Leader

Have you heard of Greta Thunberg? In many ways, she was a typical sixteen-year-old student from Sweden in 2019. But Greta was named TIME magazine's 2019 Person of the Year. She's the youngest person to ever win the award. How did she do it?

Starting in August 2018, she started camping out in front of the Swedish Parliament, holding a sign that said: 'School Strike for Climate.' Within 16 months, her movement had exploded. She addressed heads of state at the U.N., met with the Pope, debated the President of the United States and inspired 4 million others to strike alongside her on September 20, 2019.

The Unlikely Teenage Leader
Greta has done what leaders have done for centuries. She just got started early. At sixteen years old, she looked like she was twelve. She's barely five feet tall. She has Asperger's Syndrome, meaning she's emotionally different than most people. She struggles with depression. She dresses plainly and doesn't try to impress anyone. She dislikes crowds, ignores small talk, and speaks in direct, uncomplicated sentences. She cannot be distracted or flattered. She is not impressed by other people's celebrity, nor does she seem to have interest in her own growing fame. But these very qualities have helped her gain global recognition.

Wow. She sounds like a very unlikely leader.

Three Qualities that Made This Teen a Leader

1. She embraces long-term thinking.
Greta sees far into the future and cares about the world she will leave to her future children.

2. She influences the influencers.
Greta works hard to be heard. She knows change happens when other leaders get involved.

3. She is as bold as a prophet.
As a teen, with no institutional support and no one to keep her company, she kept speaking out.

Even if you don't agree with her beliefs or strategy, Greta Thunberg is an example for us. She led the largest youth movement on earth in 2019. She believes doing something—even when alone—is better than doing nothing. "Learning about climate change triggered my depression in the first place," she says. "But it was also what got me out of my depression, because there were things I could do to improve the situation. I don't have time to be depressed anymore."

Think It Over, Talk It Over

1. Do you identify with any of Greta's struggles or personal challenges?
2. What do you think motivated Greta to get involved? What sparked her action?
3. What social problem makes you angry or discouraged? What could you do about it?

To watch a video about this young leader, go to: ICantWaitBook.com

I CAN'T WAIT!

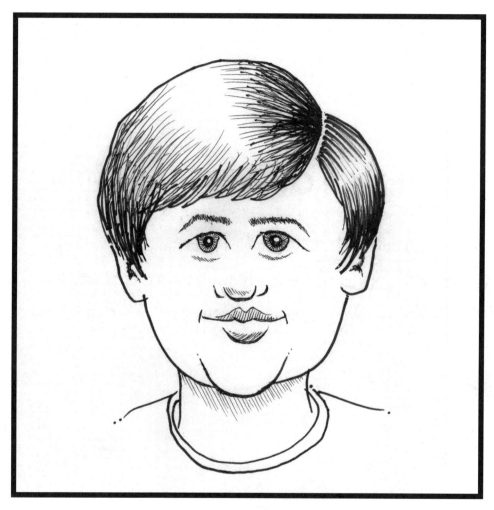

Trevor Ferrell

A Different Kind of Homework

When Trevor was eleven years old, he was doing his homework in front of the TV in his living room. He began watching a news program that revealed how many homeless people were living in his hometown of Philadelphia. These "street people" had no place to go when it was cold, and they had no food to eat. Trevor could hardly believe it.

That night at dinner, Trevor told his parents about this problem, and asked them what they could do about it. At first, his parents suggested they give money to The Union League or pray for them at bedtime that night. But Trevor wanted to do more. He talked his parents into taking him downtown in their car to look for a homeless person on the streets. They quickly found one sleeping on the sidewalk and stopped their car. Trevor got out and gave blankets for bedding to this man, who smiled and thanked him. Once Trevor returned to the car, his parents thought his appetite for helping street people might be satisfied now that he had helped someone.

But Trevor's appetite to serve people only got stronger.

He wanted to help more and more people who were homeless. Later, Trevor and his parents established a homeless shelter called "Trevor's Place" when he was a young teen. They also wrote a book by the same name, which explained what they were doing and encouraged others to do something too. The book was published in 1985.

What I Appreciate About Trevor
I got to meet Trevor when he was a teenager in 1988. Although he was humble, I asked him to speak to a large crowd of other students about what drove him to stop merely watching TV and to start doing something about the problems he saw. That is exactly why I admire Trevor:

- He didn't just feel sorry for homeless people when he saw them on TV; he did something.
- He did not stop with serving just one person; he sacrificed to find a way to serve many.
- He worked with his parents and the city of Philadelphia to create a homeless shelter.
- He eventually recruited other volunteers (both kids and adults) to help serve others.

Trevor Farrell's work was recognized by President Ronald Reagan in his 1986 State of the Union address. A TV movie dramatizing Trevor's story and titled Christmas on Division Street, aired in 1991. Pretty cool stuff.

The Bottom Line
Even as a young kid, Trevor Ferrell was an activist. He wanted to do something, not just talk about it. He even got his mom and dad involved, as well as hundreds of other people who gave their time and energy to serve food and clothes to homeless people.

He made a huge difference.

Think It Over, Talk It Over

1. Have you ever seen people hurting on TV or social media and gotten upset? What did you see?
2. Did you ever do something about a problem you spotted, even if it didn't involve you?
3. How could you take an action step about a local problem and get others involved?

To watch a video about this young leader, go to: ICantWaitBook.com

I CAN'T WAIT!

Joan of Arc

Courage Creates Commitment

Joan was a young teenage girl when she got an idea while she was praying, prompting her to help her country. She lived in France six hundred years ago, during a time when England and France were fighting the "Hundred Years War." Many lives were lost in battle when Joan felt compelled to take action, save France from their enemies, and help King Charlies return to his rightful place on the throne of her nation. A treaty signed years earlier had removed King Charles at England's request. Joan believed this was wrong and felt someone needed to help him become king again. She also felt that "someone" was her.

This was a big deal for a young teen—so big, in fact, that few people took her seriously.

She told her parents what she felt she was supposed to do, but they lovingly said she was too young to do something so big. One night, she traveled to speak to a French military commander, telling him she wanted to volunteer to help the army. He scoffed, telling her she was a young girl and should go back to her father and do what he told her to do. Joan wanted to obey her parents and leaders, but knew she was supposed to get involved right away.

She traveled to Vaucouleurs, France, a nearby stronghold for those who supported King Charles. She told a local leader, Robert De Baudricourt, that she would be happy to lead a troop of soldiers to Reims, where Charles was—to rescue him and to take him to Orleans where he could be crowned as king again. Robert didn't want to let her, but Joan persisted, and he finally gave in.

At this point, Joan made a big commitment to get the job done.

Joan's Commitment and Sacrifice
She cut her hair and put on men's clothing and armor. (She knew soldiers might not follow a teenage girl.) Even though she never killed anyone, she led the charge against the enemy, getting a band of soldiers to follow due to her bravery. When the troop encountered a wall, Joan told the French officer, "I will lead the climb over this wall."

When he replied, "You won't get anyone to follow you," Joan said, "I won't be looking back to see if anyone's following me."

That's how courageous she was.

She finally reached Charles and told him her plan. Against the advice of most of his counselors, Charles granted her request. Joan set out to fend off the Siege of Orléans in March of 1429, dressed in white armor and riding a white horse. She forced the enemy to retreat and was able to keep her promise.

Charles was restored to his role as king. A year later, Joan was captured and killed by the enemy. Legend has it that before they burned her body, she yelled out: "Do not pity me for dying for this cause. Pity the person who has no cause for which they're willing to die."

Think It Over, Talk It Over

1. What is your favorite part of Joan's story? What could you apply to your life?
2. Did you ever feel strongly about something, and it sparked you to take action?
3. What is a noble cause that you care about? Do you have the courage to respond?

To watch a video about this young leader, go to: ICantWaitBook.com

I CAN'T WAIT!

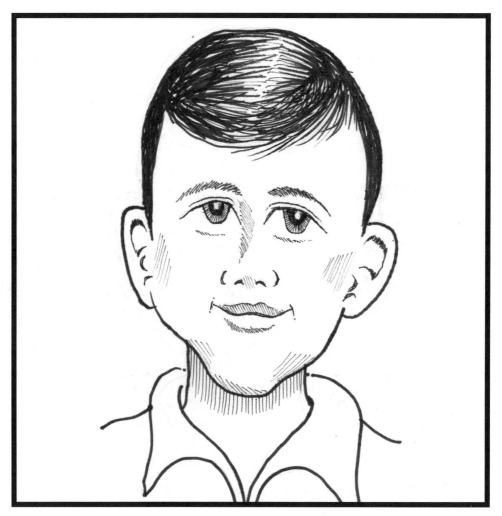

Jimmy Henson

The Socks that Talk

Jimmy was born in Greenville, Mississippi, in 1936. As a kid, he wasn't like the other boys in town. Instead of going outside to play pickup basketball or little league baseball, he preferred playing in his own room, alone. Jimmy's older brother Paul regularly encouraged him to join the other kids playing in the neighborhood, and once in a while, Jimmy did. Usually, however, he preferred to get lost in his imagination playing with designs he made up in his bedroom. He even created his own toys.

At one point, his creations got a little strange.

Jimmy's mom and dad began seeing him playing with his socks. Yep. You read that correctly. He loved creating little characters out of his stockings or socks, making them come alive with personalities and attitudes, giving them names and even giving them voices. At first, this seemed peculiar to his entire family, but fortunately for Jimmy, his parents, Paul and Betty, decided to stop trying to make him do something he didn't want to do, and instead, they focused on what he loved doing. So, they bought him more socks. Lots of them.

Over the years, Jimmy got very good at developing "little people" out of his socks and later was captivated when he saw puppeteers on TV. He remembered the arrival of the family's first television as "the biggest event of his adolescence." His favorites were programs featuring the early television puppets of Burr Tillstrom on Kukla, Fran and Ollie and Bil and Cora Baird.

He was hooked.

But Jimmy took the idea of puppets to a new level. His socks later turned into a genre of puppeteering that he called "Muppets." And we know this young man as Jim Henson. Millions have enjoyed his characters like Kermit the Frog, Miss Piggy, Gonzo, and dozens of others. One of his firsts, Ralph (a piano playing dog), appeared on the Ed Sullivan Show in September 1966.

Later, the Children's Television Workshop decided to create an educational program for kids. They asked Henson and his staff to work full-time on Sesame Street, a children's program for public television that premiered on National Educational Television on November 10, 1969. Part of the show was set aside for a series of funny, colorful puppet characters living on Sesame Street, including Grover, Bert and Ernie, Cookie Monster, Oscar the Grouch, and Big Bird. These characters were all early versions of Jim Henson's new universe called Muppets.

Later, The Muppet Show was a regular program on TV and The Muppet Movie was released in 1979, which led to several other Muppet movies in the 1980s. And it all began with Jim's socks.

I'm so glad Jimmy chose to do something different than the other kids were doing.

Think It Over, Talk It Over

1. What did you enjoy most about Jimmy's story? Do you relate to any of it?
2. Do you feel different than your classmates? In what way?
3. What could you create that may be enjoyable or beneficial for others?

To watch a video about this young leader, go to: ICantWaitBook.com

I CAN'T WAIT!

Malala Yousafzai

Turning Tragedy into Triumph

Malala is a different sort of name for a very different sort of girl. She grew up in Pakistan and was raised by loving parents who really believed in her. This gave her unusual courage.

She needed that courage because Malala lived in a place where life was stressful, especially for girls. Some people in her country didn't believe that girls should have the privilege of getting an education. Fortunately, her father started a school that allowed girls to attend.

While attending this school, the Taliban (a terrorist group) began attacking schools that allowed female students to attend. This obviously made life even more stressful. Malala had to decide whether to stand up to such threats or just be silent. She chose to handle her stress with courage. She focused on a girl's right to an education rather than her stress. In 2009, she gave a speech to encourage everyone to recognize that girls deserve an education, just like anyone else. The title of her speech was: "How Dare the Taliban Take Away My Basic Right to Education?"

At that point, the Taliban began to make death threats on this young teen.

Turning Tragedy into Triumph
On October 9, 2012, tragedy happened. When fifteen-year old Malala was riding home from school, a masked gunman boarded the bus and demanded to know which girl was Malala. When her friends looked toward her, her location was clear. The gunman fired at her, hitting Malala on the left side of her head.

The bullet then traveled down her neck. Two other girls were also injured in the attack. The shooting left Malala in critical condition, and many thought she would die. She was treated at a military hospital and then later was flown to England for further treatment. Miraculously, Malala did not die. In fact, she returned to school in England by March 2013.

- Most thought Malala would not survive, but she did.
- Then, most thought she would never return to school, but she did.
- Later, most thought she could not continue as an education activist, but she did.

The shooting resulted in a massive outpouring of support for Malala in the years afterward.

Following this horrible attack, Malala said that "the terrorists thought that they would change our aims and stop our ambitions, but nothing changed in my life except this: weakness, fear and hopelessness died. Strength, power and courage were born."

Nine months after being shot by the Taliban, Malala gave a speech at the United Nations on her sixteenth birthday in 2013. She highlighted her focus on education and women's rights, urging world leaders to change their policies. Believe it or not, in 2014, Malala became the youngest recipient to win a Nobel Peace Prize at the age of seventeen. And she was only getting started.

Think It Over, Talk It Over

1. Did you notice how Malala dealt with her trauma? What was her repeated response?
2. What impresses you most about her story?
3. How could you apply the same courage to deal with your stress?

To watch a video about this young leader, go to: ICantWaitBook.com

I CAN'T WAIT!

Ayush Kumar

Never Too Young

Ayush Kumar's parents give him just thirty minutes of screen time a week. Typically, he fills that time with videos and games. Wanting to guard him from the negative impact of technology, his parents believed their fourth grader was too young for a phone.

His parents noticed, however, that their son had loved coding since he was four years old. In fact, sometimes Ayush would use his thirty minutes of tech time to learn instead of to be entertained. So, mom and dad stayed on the lookout for opportunities for their son to do something constructive with his skills. When his dad heard about Apple's Worldwide Developers Conference, he told Ayush about it. He said, "Ayush, you're too young to enter their annual contest, but you could try to develop something and see what they say."

And that's exactly what Ayush Kumar did.

He developed a physics-based app with a catapult lever that enables users to release a projectile. It's quite impressive. Apple not only made an exception to let this ten-year-old into the contest, but Ayush won the contest— against people who were much older than he is—and was awarded a college scholarship!

So, what can we learn from him?

First, Ayush has grown up in a world full of smart technology. It is his natural habitat. Trying new opportunities with artificial intelligence is natural. Creating something helpful with it is instinctive for many kids. Technology is something to respect and use to make the world better.

Second, a caring adult made a difference in his life (in this case, it was his dad). Ayush's father was the one who cautioned him about the boundaries of the opportunity. He told his son the contest was for people thirteen-years old or older and that he probably couldn't get in, but he challenged him to give it a shot. Ayush simply followed what his dad said.

Third, Ayush broke the rules of the contest, but delivered a better project than all the older participants. Even though other contestants complained that he was too young to be there, Ayush respectfully listened to them and then submitted to the judges' decision. No one could argue with his humble attitude that honored their verdict.

Their decision stood: Ayush shouldn't be limited by the boundaries they set. It was his intelligence and his respect that won them over.

Think It Over, Talk It Over

1. What impresses you most about the story of Ayush?
2. This smart kid also had a good heart. How did he show it to others?
3. Why do you think showing respect is so important?

To watch a video about this young leader, go to: ICantWaitBook.com

I CAN'T WAIT!

Lucy Blaylock

Lucy's Love Blankets

When Lucy Blaylock was eight years old, she considered herself a normal kid in the second grade. Except for one thing: she learned how to sew that year to make a quilt for her friend's birthday. Following the party, Lucy asked her mom if they could create a blanket to give away to a child in need. She posted the idea on social media and got sixteen messages from parents with kids who suffered from cancer, autism, school bullies, and other challenges. Lucy's mother expected her to select one of these children to give a blanket to, but Lucy couldn't choose. In fact, she cried thinking of these children who needed help, and she couldn't say "no" to any of them.

So, Lucy and her mom began sewing and finished a blanket for every one of them.

If you've never sewn a blanket or quilt before, you may not realize what a slow process it is. You can't create a blanket in ten minutes, and then move on to the next one. It takes patience and persistence, especially when you work for a long time and you don't see much progress. It's easy to become impatient. Lucy was excited about giving these gifts away, and it was hard to keep working without reaching the goal after a day or two.

Along the way, Lucy learned self-control.

This is a virtue that's difficult to develop in our day where things are "instant access" and "on demand." But those who have it do great things. Psychologists call it impulse control, and it's the ability to stay steady, to manage your emotions and keep going, even when you want to quit.

Instead of letting your negative emotions control you, you decide to control them. Lucy learned that emotions make a good servant, but a bad master. She and her mom decided to focus on the excitement of giving a blanket to someone who really needed it, instead of the pain of sewing one stitch at a time, day in and day out. Lucy's compassion outweighed her impatience—and she continued until she reached each of her goals.

Her story was featured on ABC's television show, Good Morning America. According to the program, by age eleven, "Lucy had made five hundred blankets for kids in fourteen countries and all over the United States, spending two hours with her sewing machine for each. Every comfy spread comes with her signature hand-stitched inside a heart."

Then, during the COVID-19 pandemic, Lucy sewed 1,100 masks for kids and healthcare workers who needed them!

"It makes me excited when I think of the kids getting the package in the mail and opening it," Lucy said. "I always hope they'll know someone cares about them. It feels good to know that I'm helping all these kids feel loved."

Think It Over, Talk It Over

1. What do you think is the hardest part of making all those blankets and masks?
2. Have you ever accomplished something hard, which forced you to work patiently?
3. In your opinion, what enables people to control their emotions and keep doing a hard job?

To watch a video about this young leader, go to: ICantWaitBook.com

I CAN'T WAIT!

Marsai Martin

It All Starts with an Idea

You might have heard of Marsai Martin. For years, she was an actress on television, best known for playing Diane on ABC's Black-ish. On that show, Marsai plays a teenager in a family who goes through the normal hassles any teen goes through—tough relationships, peer pressure, learning to drive, studying for tough exams in class. You get the idea.

In real life, however, Marsai has accomplished something no one her age has achieved before. Marsai Martin broke a Guinness World Record as the youngest Hollywood executive producer to work on a major film. Yep, that's right. In 2019, at the age of fourteen, Marsai was an executive producer for the movie, Little, while also starring in the film.

"It feels crazy, honestly," Marsai said in an interview. "A world record? That's insane." She then summarized her thoughts by saying, "To be able to create a film, to star in it and be with your favorite stars, and actually seeing that entire experience was so amazing."

How Did a Teen Pull This Off?

So, how did she do this? Well, it required good creative thinking and hard work. But it also required building good relationships with lots of people along the way. At age ten, Marsai pitched the idea for her film, Little, to Black-ish producer Kenya Barris, who later served as one of the producers for Marsai's movie.

They spent hours together talking over the idea. After the pitch was accepted, Marsai began meeting other key people, getting to know them and discussing the best way to achieve the film project. After all, this was no homemade YouTube video idea. Marsai envisioned a major Hollywood motion picture. After numerous meetings with executives at Universal Pictures, Martin signed a deal with them and began working with screenwriters that year. All of this required patience and lots of friendships built over the span of four years.

No matter how big someone's talent is, people usually don't accomplish anything great alone. It requires people— even teenagers—to display a maturity about developing friendships, listening well, adjusting your original ideas a bit, and demonstrating lots of respect for others. And it requires time to cultivate those relationships. It has been said, "If you want to travel faster, travel alone. But if you want to travel further, travel together." People accomplish more when they do it with teammates who share similar values and want to accomplish the same goal.

You can find Marsai Martin in the 2021 edition of the Guinness World Records book. She has now launched a production company, Genius Productions, and is working on new films.

Think It Over, Talk It Over

1. What was the most amazing part of Marsai Martin's story to you?
2. Why do you think her ability to build relationships with peers and adults was important?
3. To reach your goals, where do you need to grow in your relationship building skills?

To watch a video about this young leader, go to: ICantWaitBook.com

I CAN'T WAIT!

Julio Rios Cantu

Inventing Eva

When Julio Rios Cantu was thirteen years old, his mother contracted breast cancer. The young teen didn't fully understand his mom's struggle, but he watched her battle cancer until she had to undergo surgery to have both breasts removed. That was enough to get this student from Monterrey, Mexico, interested in the issue of cancer.

Without a teacher prompting him, Julio decided to find out how big this problem was. He soon discovered that breast cancer is a gigantic hardship for women worldwide. About one in eight women in the U.S. battle breast cancer each year. Millions struggle with it globally.

That statistic was enough to drive him to start thinking about solving this problem.

The following year, Julio made some big decisions. He thought about how much he cared for his mother and how he almost lost her due to her struggle with cancer. He knew he could go on like any normal kid—playing video games and attending school—but that didn't feel right. As he evaluated what he should do, he felt he had to do something about this terrible disease. He began choosing to use his time more wisely than he had before.

Over the next two years, he told two friends about his decision to fight breast cancer because his mom almost didn't survive her health crisis over it.

He told them, "When I was thirteen years old, my mother was diagnosed for the second time with breast cancer. The tumor went from having the dimensions of a grain of rice to that of a golf ball in less than six months. The diagnosis came too late, and my mother lost both of her breasts and, almost, her life."

Now, his friends also had a decision to make. Both chose to join forces with Julio and see what they could invent. You might say it became a sort of gigantic science project for them.

They discovered that making good choices aimed at solving a problem can do a lot.

By age eighteen, Cantu and his three friends formed the company Higia Technologies, and created a bra for women that detects cancer early. They call the invention, "Eva." Julio explained, "When there is a tumor in the breast there is more blood, more heat, so there are changes in temperature and in texture." When a woman wears this bra once a week, she can detect if warmth and blood flow are different, signaling her to go to the doctor to discover if she might have cancer.

Eva applies biosensor abilities to medical technology for early detection of cancer. Just wearing it one hour a week could save the lives of millions of people. The invention was enough for Julio to win the Global Student Entrepreneur Award winner in 2017, with a top prize of $20,000. Not bad for a teenager.

Think It Over, Talk It Over

1. What do you think went through Julio's mind to make him decide to do this project?
2. What keeps kids from making good decisions?
3. When was the last time you decided to do something important? What happened?

To watch a video about this young leader, go to: ICantWaitBook.com

I CAN'T WAIT!

Robert Heft

Earning an "A"

Did you know that our American flag, the one you see almost every day somewhere in your community, was designed by a teenager? It's true. His name was Robert Heft.

Robert saw himself as a typical high school student. But that all changed after completing a school project for his history teacher, Mr. Stanley Pratt, back in 1958. Robert was seventeen years old at the time, and Mr. Pratt gave an assignment to his class to design something that demonstrated what they had learned and enjoyed about American history.

Robert had just heard rumors that the United States might soon be adding two new states to the union: Alaska and Hawaii. Robert thought how cool it would be to design the new American flag with fifty stars on it, instead of the current one that had only forty-eight. So, he went to work, and his project turned out beautifully. He was proud to turn it in.

Imagine his letdown when Mr. Pratt gave him a B minus. Robert was disappointed because he had worked so hard and felt like he turned in an excellent assignment. That night, his mom and dad could tell he was struggling with negative emotions. So, they asked him what he was feeling. Fortunately, Robert was able to recognize he was feeling a bit frustrated and sad. As they discussed his feelings, they pondered what he could do about it.

Obviously, one option was to simply let it go. After all, Mr. Pratt was the teacher and it was his decision to give Robert a B minus.

Another option, however, would be to talk it over with Mr. Pratt. That seemed like a good way to respond to the disagreement.

Robert decided to let his negative emotions nudge him in a positive direction.

So, Robert asked to meet with his teacher after class to discuss his grade. He explained that the project was in response to a real need; that America would soon admit two more states into the Union and that they would need a flag with fifty stars. Mr. Pratt reflected, then told Robert if there was an act of Congress to select his design to be the new U.S. flag, he would change Robert's grade. The two reached an agreement. (Mr. Pratt was sure it would never happen.)

Robert sent his creation to the White House in Washington D.C. at the same time 1,500 other people from across the country had turned in their design. Robert followed up by writing twenty-one letters to President Eisenhower, and he called Congress eighteen times to follow up. Finally, his phone rang. Believe it or not, President Eisenhower actually called him to let him know Congress had chosen his design to be the official flag of the United States of America.

A confirmation letter followed that Robert showed to Mr. Pratt. His teacher raised his eyebrows and smiled. And sure enough, Mr. Pratt changed Robert's grade from a B minus to an A immediately. How cool is that?

Think It Over, Talk It Over

1. Why do you think it was important for Robert to identify what he felt when he got a B minus?
2. Are you able to recognize your emotions well? Do they ever prompt you to take action?
3. When was the last time you spotted your emotions and did something good with them?

To watch a video about this young leader, go to: ICantWaitBook.com

I CAN'T WAIT!

Kelvin Doe

Turning Trash into Treasure

Kelvin was one of many kids growing up in a difficult world. Born in Sierra Leone, Africa, his country endured a terrifying civil war, killing thousands of people and leaving many without homes, food, water, or basic living supplies. Just a few years after the war ended, many people were still just trying to survive.

At eleven years old, Kelvin decided to do more than just survive.

This eleven-year-old inventor got started on his journey to being a leader as he began looking for ways to fix local problems with technology. This was just five years after the volatile civil war ended. In the beginning, he spotted small problems that he was able to fix quickly. By age thirteen, however, he was powering neighborhood houses with batteries made from acid, soda, and a metal tin cup. It was working. People began to have hope again.

He went on to build a community radio station out of recycled parts that he powered with a generator, also made from reused metal. He began playing music and broadcast news under the name, "DJ Focus." You can imagine by this time, people began to know who this young teen was. He was one of the finalists in Global Minimum Inc.'s Innovate Salone idea competition, where Kelvin built another generator from scrap metals. People were amazed at how Kelvin could take a bunch of scraps (wood, metal, wires, plastic, cans) and make something useful out of them. And he used discarded pieces of unwanted electronics to build transmitters, generators, and batteries. It was always about solving problems and serving people.

In many ways, he turned trash into treasure.

Turning Trash into Treasure
As a result of his accomplishments, Kelvin received an invitation to the United States and became the youngest person to participate in the Visiting Innovation Fellows Program at M.I.T., a major engineering college in Boston.

Kelvin later gave a TEDx Teen speech and has lectured to college students at Harvard College. In 2013, Kelvin Doe signed a $100,000 solar project agreement with Canadian High Speed Service Provider Sierra WiFi.

Now one of Sierra Leone's most famous inventors, Kelvin owns and runs his own company K-Doe Tech, Inc., where he designs and sells consumer electronics. He's had the chance to meet various world leaders and has spoken to young people in Africa on many different platforms. Kelvin is inspiring other kids to do whatever they can now to make the world better. After all, anyone can look around and find odds and ends (scraps) that others might throw away, right? The key? Just find trash and turn it into treasure. David Sengeh, Kelvin's mentor at the MIT media lab, said: "In Sierra Leone, other young people suddenly feel they can be like Kelvin."

Think It Over, Talk It Over

1. What is most amazing to you about Kelvin's story?
2. What do you think motivated him to turn trash into treasure?
3. What is one step you could take from what you learn from Kelvin?

To watch a video about this young leader, go to: ICantWaitBook.com

I CAN'T WAIT!

Louis Braille

When Your Problem Leads to Your Purpose

Louis was born in France in 1809. When he was three years old, tragedy happened. He was accidentally blinded in one eye by an awl, a sharp tool in his father's shop. By the age of five, both of his eyes got infected and he became completely blind. Louis' parents knew they'd have to find a very different school for him to get an education. In a few years, they finally found it.

He attended the National Institute for Blind Youth in Paris. The system they used to help blind kids to read was called "sonography," created by Charles Barbier. It was designed to help the French army gain information at night when it was too dark to read words. It wasn't a bad tool; it was just too complex for blind children. Louis used this reading system for a number of years, but he found it confusing, too large and too difficult for most blind kids to learn.

There had to be a better way.

Starting at age twelve, Louis began creating his own way for blind people to read. It took him three years but he finally created a simpler method that worked brilliantly.

His system used only six dots—just enough to feel with your fingertip.

He combined these dots to create sixty-four symbols which enables a blind person to read any concept.

Believe it or not, Louis created this alphabet for the blind at age fifteen. You may have heard of it. It's named after him: the Braille system. How could a kid come up with something this amazing, even better than anything that adults had created? The answer is simple. Since Louis was blind himself:

- This gave him a great compassion for others who were blind.
- This gave him a great urgency to come up with something better.
- This gave him a great sense of diligence to finish his creation.
- This gave him a great purpose to become a teacher himself.

Louis is a fantastic example of someone who turned their problem into their purpose. His "mess" became his "message." His obstacle became his opportunity. His stumbling block became a stepping stone. How? He used an awl, the very tool that had accidentally blinded him as a toddler, to create a new system to help him read. Instead of his blindness causing him to get stuck, it caused him to get started. And the tool that wounded him now enabled him to solve a problem.

It took a few years for people to adopt this new system, which was first published in 1829 when he was still a teenager. A more complete version of it appeared in 1837 when Louis was a teacher. Believe it or not, the Braille system is still used today, and blind people all over the world read books written with this system. All thanks to a motivated teenager.

Think It Over, Talk It Over

1. How frustrating do you think it was for Louis to try to read but find it almost impossible?
2. What do you like most about his story? What's inspiring about it to you?
3. Have you ever gotten frustrated with a problem? What could you do to solve it?

To watch a video about this young leader, go to: ICantWaitBook.com

I CAN'T WAIT!

Sagen Woolrey

Hungry to Help the Hungry

Sagen considered herself an ordinary kid when she was growing up. Except for one thing: she could not stand seeing someone going hungry. It made her emotional; she got both mad and sad. By the time she turned twelve, something happened that turned an emotion into an action.

She was watching TV one day and saw a commercial about community service. Although she was still young, she wanted to volunteer and do something that would make a difference. She was worried about kids who didn't have food to eat at home.

"I wondered where children who depend on the free lunch program at school could eat lunch during the summer," Sagen said. "The more I thought about it, the more I worried about my friends in need."

Sagen had to do something. The more she thought about her friends being really hungry, the more passionate she became. She could not sit still. Sagen and her mother visited the director at a local soup kitchen where she learned how a person like her could help serve those who are hungry. This soup kitchen director helped Sagen do what was necessary to get her idea off the ground:

1. She organized a plan.
2. She prepared menus.
3. She solicited donations for food and money.
4. She got permission from both a food bank and her church to launch her idea.

She started "The Kid's Kitchen," a free lunch program for hungry kids, at age twelve. Every Wednesday, all summer long, Sagen and the other students she recruited provided food for any kid who didn't have enough food. She coordinated more than 120 volunteers to serve, all kids between the ages of eight and twelve years old. It was a food program run by kids, for kids.

You Either Organize or You Agonize
If you were to talk to Sagen about The Kid's Kitchen, she would tell you it was a team effort that required lots of planning and organizing. But she felt she had to do it; she was in agony over how many kids were hungry and needed food. She realized she could either agonize or organize.

Along with providing lunches, Sagen used part of her donated funds to buy toiletries and school supplies for the needy children who come to her "kitchen." The Kid's Kitchen served more than 3,200 people in her community in the first two summers it existed. Sagen said. "I believe that if one person is fed and not hungry, it is a big accomplishment. I think we are all responsible for each other."

Think It Over, Talk It Over

1. Have you ever seen someone do something big for someone else? What was it?
2. What is cool about this story? Is it inspiring how Sagen organized The Kid's Kitchen?
3. Do you like to organize? What have you organized that helped get something done?

To watch a video about this young leader, go to: ICantWaitBook.com

I CAN'T WAIT!

De'monte Love

Not Too Young to Lead

You may not remember Hurricane Katrina, but I sure do. In fact, most adults do. It was a terrifying hurricane that blasted through New Orleans, Louisiana (and other southern states) in 2005. It was one of the worst storms in my memory.

- The winds blew over cars and trees.
- The power went out as the streets were flooded.
- Water gushed in from the ocean and filled the houses.
- People tried to escape the damage and families got separated.

People became refugees, which is a name for anyone who is displaced, trying to escape, and has no home. They are trying to survive as they flee from a dangerous situation. One group of refugees stood out in the chaos. They were all children. They were holding hands. Three of the children were about two years old, and one was wearing only diapers. A three-year-old girl, who wore colorful barrettes on the ends of her braids, had her younger brother with her. The oldest was a six-year-old who was holding a five-month old baby. He spoke for all of them. The group of six followed him as if he was their leader. He told the police his name was De'monte Love.

But wait a minute. How could a six-year old end up being in charge of six babies?

Part of the answer is simple. When the hurricane raged inland, chaos broke out. People were running everywhere, and some were carried away by the water.

The day De'monte led his rescue, parents had reported 220 missing children and that number was growing. Parents could not find their kids. De'Monte was just trying to help these kids get to safety, to find help and eventually get them back to their parents.

Years later, De'Monte explained his thoughts at the time:

- He was scared but knew he had to stay calm.
- He knew he was the oldest kid in the group and felt they needed help.
- He believed he had to step up and lead the way.

The escape began as De'Monte was with his mother and a crowd of other people on top of the roof of an apartment building. When a rescue helicopter arrived, there wasn't room for everyone. His mom was left behind, but the pilot said he'd be right back. Sadly, he was unable to return. As they were separated, De'Monte's mother gave her son clear instructions to take care of his baby brother. Well, De'Monte did more than that. Alone, he took care of all six kids, each one younger than him. His story was translated into a children's book, called Heroes All Around.

De'Monte Love's mother finally got reunited with her son who led this group of children to safety after Hurricane Katrina. Can you guess her name? Her name is Catrina.

Think It Over, Talk It Over

1. What do you think helped De'Monte to be such a good leader at age six?
2. When have you seen people achieve amazing goals, more than what seems possible?
3. Have you ever had to do something that you felt was too much for you to handle?

To watch a video about this young leader, go to: ICantWaitBook.com

I CAN'T WAIT!

Sonia Sotomayor

Tough Times Made Her Tough

Sonia is an unlikely hero. But she's definitely a hero. Sonia Sotomayor was diagnosed with Type 1 diabetes when she was seven years old, at a time when diabetics were not expected to survive very long. She would have to get shots every day. Her parents planned to handle those insulin injections, but her mom worked long hours as a nurse and her father died when she was nine. So, she learned to give herself shots. At an early age, Sonia realized that life was going to be tough, but Sonia's battle against diabetes actually drove her to succeed.

When her father died, it motivated her to work harder. Although Sonia was smart, her family was poor and her mom didn't know how to help her succeed. Yet contending with challenges didn't stop Sotomayor's rise—in fact, hardships helped forge her strong character and gave her determination when she failed. She said, "This drove me in a way that perhaps nothing else might have to accomplish as much as I could as early as possible."

Sonia got accepted to Princeton University, an Ivy League college, in 1972. She was different since most of the other students grew up wealthy. While she was still getting used to college life, she also had to deal with discrimination from the students and alumni; many were hostile to the women and minorities their school had recently begun to admit, sentiments they freely shared in letters to the school paper. But when her grades fell short in her first year, she refused to believe she "didn't belong" at Princeton, as some had told her. She studied harder and turned her poor grades into amazing ones. She ended up graduating at the top of her class.

How Did Sonia's Tough Times Make Her Better?

Everything she endured early on actually made Sonia more determined to succeed and to help others succeed. When we think about the experiences she had, we see what shaped her:

- Growing up with diabetes gave her compassion for others with diseases.
- Growing up as a girl helped her understand how it feels to be overlooked for a job.
- Growing up as a minority gave her resolve to fight against workplace discrimination.
- Growing up poor helped her to enforce laws that gave everyone opportunities for work.

Believe it or not, Sonia Sotomayor felt empathy for others who struggle when she was just nine years old. She began advocating for equal rights for everyone as a teenager. She began fighting against workplace discrimination at age twenty-one. Sonia was a pioneer even as a young person who was helping people to have an equal chance to reach their dreams. She doesn't think everyone should be guaranteed equal results, just equal opportunities. Sonia is only the third woman and the first Hispanic to become a Supreme Court justice. She was inspired to write a children's book, "Just Ask! Be Different, Be Brave, Be You," about the value of respecting people's differences.

Think It Over, Talk It Over

1. What inspires you most about Sonia's story? Do you have anything in common with her?
2. How do you think Sonia's difficult life gave her confidence instead of making her scared?
3. Did you ever have to overcome being anxious or afraid? What gave you confidence?

To watch a video about this young leader, go to: ICantWaitBook.com

I CAN'T WAIT!

Oprah Winfrey

She Has a Way with Words

Oprah was born on January 29, 1954, in a very poor area of rural Mississippi. She grew up there, but also in Milwaukee, Wisconsin and Nashville, Tennessee. In each place, she lived in poverty with family members who were often abusive and discouraging. When you hear her entire story, it is difficult to believe she became so strong, so rich, and so famous as an adult.

- She lived in poverty, raised by a teenage mother in multiple locations.
- For years, she wore old clothes made out of potato sacks.
- Her classmates made fun of her as a young girl because of how she looked.
- Family members abused her for years, and once she even got pregnant.
- She was sent to live with others in different states since her mom was so poor.

But something happened inside of her as each of these difficulties took place. She recognized she would need to look inside of herself and find a way to survive. She would need to find inward courage. She would need to build her own faith in God, and she'd need to discover her gifts and talents since others were unable to provide for her.

It didn't take long to see she had a way with words.

Words Became Her Way to Get Ahead
Her grandmother taught Oprah to read before the age of three and took her to church, where she was nicknamed "The Preacher" for her ability to recite Bible verses.

In fact, ever since she could talk, Oprah was on stage. As a child, she played games interviewing her corncob doll and the crows on the backyard fence.

Her mother finally sent her to live with her father, Vernon Winfrey, in Nashville, and Oprah would stay there until she graduated high school. Oprah thrived in school. She was an honors student, voted Most Popular Girl, and she placed second in the nation in dramatic interpretation for her high school speech team. She soon landed a job in radio and was hired to do the news part-time her senior year of high school and first two years of college. By nineteen, she was a co-anchor for the local evening news. How did she get into college being so poor? You guessed it. She won a speech contest, which gave her a full scholarship to Tennessee State University. What did she study?

Communication, of course!

Oprah's personal style led to her hosting a daytime talk show. After boosting that Chicago show to first place, she launched her own production company. Over time, Oprah Winfrey was voted "the most influential woman in the world" many times. And it all started with finding her talent.

Think It Over, Talk It Over

1. How do you think noticing her skill with words well helped Oprah through hard times?
2. Look at Oprah's story again. Talk about how each achievement led to a new opportunity.
3. What are your primary gifts and talents? Have you ever put them to the test? How?

To watch a video about this young leader, go to: ICantWaitBook.com

I CAN'T WAIT!

Peyton Robertson

The Sandless Sandbag

When he was eleven years old, Peyton Robertson watched Hurricane Sandy devastate the U.S. coastline on TV in 2012. He also watched rescue workers try to stop the flooding waters that gushed everywhere, ruining houses, cars, and roads. These workers positioned sandbags in dozens of places, doing their best to stop the damage, but they couldn't keep up. It was a frightening hurricane that left thousands trying to recover from the destruction.

Peyton was particularly intrigued at how sandbags were failing to stop the flooding. Sandbags couldn't prevent the water from penetrating. He wondered why someone hadn't invented something more effective by then. When he spoke to his parents at dinner and to some friends later about the problem, no one had an answer. No one had a better solution.

This made Peyton begin to ask himself, "What could I do?"

Many people would have said, "You're just a young kid. You can't do anything to solve this big problem." But Peyton knew differently. He recognized who he was: he had a good mind, he was very curious, and he loved science. He knew he could more than anyone expected of him. So, what did he do? He invented a sandbag with no sand.

Peyton is from Ft. Lauderdale, Florida, so he's seen a few storms and floods even as a kid. It's what drove him to design his new protection against floods, hurricanes, and other disasters. He calls it the Sandless Operational Sandbag (SOS).

Here is his flow of thought:

- Conventional sandbags are heavy to transport, and they leave gaps.
- People needed a lighter sandbag that could expand to fill those gaps.
- What if he made a bag with a combination of salt and polymer inside?
- The bag would be doused with water before use so the polymer expands.
- The mixture makes the bag light, easy to store, and more effective.

It makes sense, doesn't it? What's cool is...it works. Peyton could see the different problems that needed to be solved and developed a solution that others couldn't see since they were limited by the way things have always been done. (We've been using sandbags since the eighteenth century.) In his own way, Peyton analyzed our current sandbags, saw why they weren't getting the job done, and invented a bag that does. (It's not that someone had never thought about using fixtures besides sandbags, but his version was new.) I love how Peyton didn't feel he was too young or inexperienced to solve this huge problem. He knew what he could do, and he did it.

His invention earned him the title of "America's Top Young Scientist" in 2013.

Think It Over, Talk It Over

1. Why do you think Payton got curious instead of scared when he saw the flood problem?
2. Do you know a student who solved a huge problem, even when they were young? Who?
3. Have you ever felt smart enough to solve a big problem? What's a problem in your community you could help solve?

To watch a video about this young leader, go to: ICantWaitBook.com

I CAN'T WAIT!

Jim Casey

Find a Need and Fill

Jim Casey was born in a small town called Pickhandle Gulch, in Nevada in 1888. As a child, Jim's dad passed away, leaving him, his mother Annie, his two brothers, and one sister to survive on their own. They moved to Seattle to find work, and it was there that Jim saw the bustling streets of a big city, reacting to the Klondike Gold Rush that began some years earlier in the area.

Moving from a small town to a big city with lots of people, lots of noise, and so many desperate folks hunting for gold created a lot of stress for Jim. It was all so new, and he was just a teenager. His mom knew the best way for her kids to get through this tough time was to find a way to help others. She spoke to her children about looking for problems to solve and about serving others with their talents. Her message to her kids was: Find a need and fill it. As a teen in 1907, Jim spotted something curious. He saw the increasing demand for telegrams since most people didn't own a phone yet. Thanks to the gold rush, folks were hungry to communicate.

Suddenly, Jim and his friend Claude Ryan had an idea.

With one bicycle between them and one hundred dollars they borrowed from a friend, the two teenagers started their own telegram delivery service, the American Messenger Company.

They soon operated out of a tavern basement with Jim and Claude manning the phone requests, while Jim's brother George and a few other teenagers delivered notes on foot or by bike. Jim thought maybe this idea could both help other people and help him manage his own stress.

And the idea took off.

A few years later, the young men merged with a rival company and began using a Model-T Ford to deliver not only telegrams, but any package that needed delivering. Soon, they added motorcycles and cars to get the job done. By 1919, they began delivering packages to other cities besides Seattle and saw the potential for a nationwide company. It was then they changed their name to United Parcel Service, or UPS.

My guess is—you've noticed their big brown delivery trucks in your neighborhood.

"Casey and Ryan's company that started so humbly is now worth approximately $81 billion with annual revenue at over $50 billion; employing just under half a million workers in 200 countries; delivering over 3.8 billion packages and documents a year. It is the largest postal delivery service in the world. Amazing what $100, some elbow grease, and a bit of ingenuity can do."

And to think it began with a couple of motivated teenagers and a little stress.

Think It Over, Talk It Over

1. Do you sometimes get overwhelmed or stressed out like Jim Casey did?
2. Why do you think it can be wise to overcome your stress by serving other people?
3. How could you fight being anxious or stressful by focusing on others?

To watch a video about this young leader, go to: ICantWaitBook.com

I CAN'T WAIT!

Dasia Taylor

When Her Talent Met a Problem

Several years ago, while attending class, high school student Dasia Taylor got an idea. In AP Human Geography class, Dasia learned that one of the leading causes of death in developing countries is post-surgical infections, often from routine surgical procedures—and she knew she had to do something about it.

Mothers often got infections after giving birth, especially when doing a cesarean section. This caught Taylor's attention. In some African nations, she learned, up to 20 percent of women who give birth by C-section later develop surgical site infections. These infections are dangerous and can often lead to death. This information, along with the challenge from her teacher to submit a project for a statewide science fair, was enough to spring Dasia into action. She felt she had to help solve this problem.

She began working on the project in October 2019, which meant that when the COVID-19 pandemic hit just a few months later, she had to continue her project while attending virtual classes. Her teacher at Iowa City West High School even allowed her to come into the labs at the school after hours alone to work on her project further.

Dasia's Big Idea
Here was her idea: Dasia "had read about sutures coated with a conductive material that can sense the status of a wound by changes in electrical resistance," but these only worked where technology is present.

So, Dasia began to experiment with less "smart" methods for sutures to detect infection, and she found one: beet juice. Dasia learned that human skin is naturally acidic, with a pH around five. When a wound becomes infected, however, its pH goes up to about nine. "I found that beets changed color at the perfect pH point," Taylor said in an interview. Bright red beet juice turns dark purple at a pH of nine. "That's perfect for an infected wound." She combined beet juice with the perfect thread for sutures, and her invention was born.

Dasia Taylor has won several science awards for her project in the years since she first began work on her idea. She was even named one of forty finalists in the Regeneron Science Talent Search, one of the country's oldest and most prestigious science and math competitions for high school seniors. But to Dasia, these awards pale in comparison to her true goal: helping protect women from infections. She is now pursuing a patent for her invention and working to mass produce a portable and effective way to use these sutures around the globe.

You might say that without even trying, Dasia became a leader. What she did was see a need, identify her own gifts, and act. We naturally gain influence when we solve problems and serve people.

Think It Over, Talk It Over

1. Have you ever taken a class that sparked an idea for you to create or invent?
2. What's the most common reason for you to spring into action to solve problems?
3. What can you learn from Dasia's story?

To watch a video about this young leader, go to: ICantWaitBook.com

I CAN'T WAIT!

Beau Jessup

The Power of a Name

One significant reality Generation Z brings with them as they grow into adulthood is an intuition on where culture is heading and how to capitalize on it. I've seen this time and again. Older adults can get locked into the way everything used to work and not see some opportunities.

We need the vision of Beau Jessup.

Beau is a little like any other teenager from the U.K. except for one reality—she's making hundreds of thousands of dollars and funding her way through college by naming Chinese babies. She was just a teenager when she found a need she could meet—and boy, did she.

It all started when Beau was fifteen and traveling with her father to China. When one of his business associates, Mrs. Wang, asked for help in giving an English name to her three-year-old daughter, Beau felt honored and surprised. "It seemed like a really important thing to do," she recalls. Wanting to choose an "appropriate" name, Beau asked Mrs. Wang to share a little more about her hopes for her daughter. Most of all, said Wang, she wanted people to be surprised by the things her daughter could achieve. So, after careful thought, Jessup suggested "Eliza," inspired by the fictionalized heroine from My Fair Lady, Eliza Doolittle. Wang was delighted, Beau said, and went on to explain the significance of having an English name for people who are Chinese.

It was something many parents wanted.

That year, 2015, marked the end of the "one child" policy in China and the birthrate rose almost 8 percent. Almost eighteen million new babies were born, and many families needed an English name. It was then Beau decided to launch "Special Name," a website that would enable Chinese parents to insert five attributes or hopes for their child through her site, and internal algorithms would help them select a perfect name. Six months later, she had made more than $60,000 naming 200,000 babies. Since then, she's named a total of 677,900 babies and generated an estimated $400,000 that goes toward paying for college, investing in property and, of course, paying back the loan her dad gave her, with interest. I believe this is a picture of the future. Like many teens:

- Beau saw an opportunity she could participate in and seize.
- Beau utilized technology to not only respond to one need but to many needs.
- Beau got passionate about it, which gave her the self-discipline to solve the problem.

Beau is part of a generation of kids that feels inspired by that smartphone in their hands. It enables them to make things happen and not wait for an adult to do something or even for permission from an adult to do something. She's already succeeding as a young entrepreneur.

Think It Over, Talk It Over

1. How would you have felt if a stranger asked you to help name her baby?
2. What do you think gave Beau the discipline to build a website and serve so many people?
3. Have you ever had someone ask you to help them? What have you done for others?

To watch a video about this young leader, go to: ICantWaitBook.com

I Can't Wait!

Avi Schiffmann

Getting the Story Straight

You may remember how scary life was in the Spring of 2020. A pandemic broke out and kids all over the world were sent home so they wouldn't catch the COVID-19 virus. Two discoveries made that year especially frightening:

First, millions of people worldwide died from this sinister infection by the end of the year. It was hard to know how easily you could catch it or if you'd have any symptoms.

Second, there were many people declaring so many contrary facts about the disease. It was hard to know who to believe and where the coronavirus would spread next.

When school went virtual for two months, one student decided to do something besides play video games and waste time. He loved science and he loved technology—so he thought he might just be a perfect person to help those who were scared. He took "inventory" of his resources and talent and decided on a great way to invest his time. This teenager created a website that tracked the coronavirus and became one of the most vital resources for people seeking accurate and updated numbers on the pandemic. The URL is nCoV2019.live.

It was seventeen-year-old Avi Schiffmann, a high school junior from Mercer Island outside Seattle, who started the site in late December 2019, when COVID-19 had not yet been detected outside of China.

By March 2020 (when all of us were sent home to quarantine), the site had been visited by tens of millions, from every country on Earth. It tracked deaths, numbers of cases locally and globally, and provided an interactive map, information on the disease, and a Twitter feed.

The resource updated every minute or so, and pulled information from the World Health Organization, the Centers for Disease Control, and elsewhere. Avi doesn't claim to be a hero—just a teen who knew his talents, saw what others desperately needed and chose to use his gifts and smarts to solve problems and serve people.

What Makes This Story Helpful for Us
Avi doesn't claim to be a genius, but he does recognize he is special in the gifts and ambition he possesses. He took the gifts he had inside and used them to meet a need millions of people had: up-to-date information on the biggest problem our world faced in 2020. Yet his unique qualities are no more special than yours. You have unique gifts inside, you are smart in specific areas, you have passion for certain topics, and you'll feel a drive to accomplish particular future goals.

- Avi had a talent to understand technology. What do you think your talent is?
- Avi had a passion for problem solving. Do you feel passionate about anything?
- Avi was smart in science. What are the subjects or issues in which you're smart?
- Avi had an ambition to build a website to help fearful people. What is your ambition?

Think It Over, Talk It Over

1. What impresses you most about Avi's initiative?
2. Review the four questions on the last page and talk about them. What pops up in your mind?
3. How can you use your time better to do something that solves problems and serves people?

To watch a video about this young leader, go to: ICantWaitBook.com

I CAN'T WAIT!

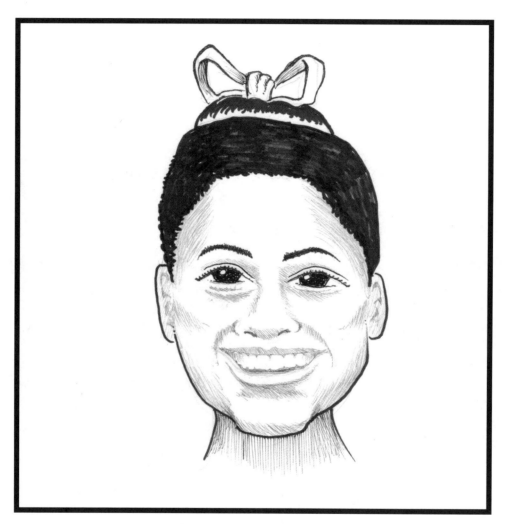

Simone Biles

Born to Perform

Simone is a girl who just wouldn't give up until she reached her goals. She was born in Columbus, Ohio, but grew up with her grandparents near Houston, Texas. When she was six years old, she went on a field trip to Bannon's Gymnastix complex to watch athletes competing in gymnastics and suddenly realized that's what she wanted to do.

She signed up and stayed at that sports complex for eleven years, perfecting her ability on the balance beam, the uneven bars, the vault, and the floor exercise. Her coach, Aimee Boorman, encouraged her and was amazed at how Simone pushed herself to try such difficult routines, some of which no female gymnast had done before. When she was thirteen, Simone entered the Junior Olympic National Championship and won a gold and a bronze medal in 2010. A year later, she was ready to enter the elite level of competition, with older, more experienced athletes. She wasn't sure how she would do against such tough competition, but she had to find out. Less than two years later, she dominated the sport.

Simone realized at sixteen years old, she was competing against some very strong and talented athletes. In fact, they were the best in the world. So, she knew that even if she couldn't add any talent to her body, she could certainly work harder than anyone else.

- She would control what she could control and not worry about anything else.
- She would focus on her work and her thoughts, not on her feelings or her opponents.

- She reminded herself of who she was and believed she had what it took to succeed.

In 2013, her first year as a senior competitor, the four-foot nine-inch Biles won the all-around title at her first world gymnastics championships, becoming the first African American woman to claim the title. Following that year, Simone Biles just kept on winning medals and championships. At the 2015 world championships, she completed her hat trick of all-around titles. Those wins brought her career total to fourteen world championship medals, the most ever earned by a U.S. gymnast, male or female. In addition, her ten world championship gold medals were the most won by a female gymnast in the sport's history.

Biles was a favorite entering the 2016 Olympics in Rio de Janeiro. She lived up to expectations, leading the United States to gold in the team event and then winning the individual all-around. Due to the COVID-19 pandemic, no major events were held in 2020, but it had no effect on Biles. At the 2021 U.S. Classic, she became the first female gymnast to land the sport's most difficult vault, the Yurchenko double pike. This is what set her apart: her consistency, her energetic personality, and the high degree of difficulty she incorporated into her routines.

Think It Over, Talk It Over

1. Why is it important to believe in yourself when you need to work hard at a goal?
2. What do you think Simone Biles was telling herself before she competed?
3. When have you had to believe in yourself in order to try something difficult?

To watch a video about this young leader, go to: ICantWaitBook.com

I Can't Wait!

The Kids Who Climbed Mount Everest

A Mountaintop Experience

We first read about a teenage girl named Malavath Poorna in 2014. She was only thirteen when she became the youngest female to ever climb Mount Everest. It is an amazing story. Mount Everest is 29,029 feet high and stands as the tallest mountain in the world. It is the dream of any serious mountain climber to scale Everest and reach the top. But it is rare. Over three hundred people have died trying to climb this intimidating mountain—due to the harsh conditions, freezing temperatures, icy winds, and steep inclines. But Malavath was determined after joining a training organization that prepared her to climb mountains. She continues to visit schools across India to encourage students to follow their dreams. This courageous Indian girl has inspired many.

In fact, five other Indians were inspired enough by Malavath Poorna that they did it too.

In 2018, forty-seven teens were selected to train to climb Everest, but only ten made it through the ten months of training. All of them tried to climb the gigantic Mount Everest. But only five of them made it to the top: Manisha, Parmesh, Vikas, Soyam, and Kavidas. Most of them came from small towns and villages and had never dreamed of doing something so difficult. A year before, none of these students had ever traveled beyond their hometown.

Even more amazing is a kid named Jordan Romero.

In fourth grade, he saw a picture of the highest mountain on each continent. He asked his dad, "Why don't we climb all of these mountains?" After lots of training, that's exactly what they did. He climbed the first at ten years old and climbed Mount Everest when he was just thirteen years old! He's the youngest ever to do it.

Do you know the most important skill all of these kids learned?

It was to control their thoughts and emotions. It took eighteen months for Malavath to climb Everest. It took this team of five just ten months to climb it. Their impulse almost every day was to stop. To surrender to the low oxygen levels or the high winds. I am sure their minds played tricks on them. A few said they had hallucinations. But anything worth doing is likely going to be hard. No one accidentally climbs a mountain.

- They had to control their feelings.
- They had to resist the temptation to seek comfort.
- They had committed to taking one step at a time until they reached the summit.

Almost anyone who has accomplished something hard has learned to control their own thoughts. They learned to tell their bodies and minds what to do, not just to follow their feelings or emotions. The truth is—the hardest person to lead is yourself. And these five climbers did just that.

Think It Over, Talk It Over

1. What is most amazing to you when you think about the story of these teenagers?
2. What's the hardest thing you've ever tried? Did you succeed? What happened?
3. What lessons can we learn from this story? Where can you apply those lessons?

To watch a video about this young leader, go to: ICantWaitBook.com

I CAN'T WAIT!

Kenton Lee

The Shoe That Grows

When Kenton was a college student, he visited East Africa and spent time in Kenya working with younger children. One day, Kenton had a "light bulb moment." As he walked next to a young girl, he noticed her shoes were way too small for her feet. The girl had to cut open the front of her shoes in order to let her toes stick out. In this moment, Kenton got an inspiration: what if someone could create a shoe that lasted for years and expand as the person grows?

That's when he began working on "The Shoe That Grows."

This was the start of a six-year process for Kenton, with lots of ups and downs, successes and failures. His journey required lots of patience, resolve, and ingenuity. He tried to give the idea away to a major shoe company—but no one was interested or wanted to help. Instead of giving up, Kenton decided to work on the invention himself. He tried to create a shoe by himself in his garage, but he didn't do a very good job. Creating something new took a lot of patience and determination.

Finally, he got some help from a small shoe design company.

These people helped Kenton's idea become a reality. It took a year, but they created a prototype he was able to try out on kids who needed shoes. He and his friends tested one hundred pairs of shoes in four different schools in Kenya. When the experiment worked, he then worked with a factory to make their first batch of three thousand pairs of these "shoes that grow" as the kids grow.

How Does the Shoe Work?

The shoe is made of leather, rubber, and Velcro straps. It is designed to adjust as your foot gets bigger. In fact, the shoe adjusts in three different places—the width, the length, and the top—and can grow up to five sizes before you need a new pair. The bottom just unfolds as you need it to, and suddenly you have a shoe that perfectly fits your foot. It grows when you grow.

It is a game changer for poor kids who often have to walk barefoot when they outgrow their shoes and suffer from soil-transmitted diseases. Believe it or not, 1.5 billion people suffer from soil-based diseases and parasites that can make them sick and even kill them. When they catch a disease, they miss school, leaving them without an education and unable to help their family.

Kenton started a non-profit organization called Because International, and he and his team now create different products that serve people, alleviate poverty, keep kids stay healthy and in school, and offer jobs to people who want to help create the products, like these shoes. They've now given over 350,000 pairs of shoes to kids in one hundred countries around the world.

Think It Over, Talk It Over

1. What do you like most about Kenton's story?
2. What lessons can we learn from this story? Where can you apply those lessons?
3. Have you ever tried to solve a problem with a creative solution?

To watch a video about this young leader, go to: ICantWaitBook.com

I CAN'T WAIT!

Six Teens in Nashville

Respond, Don't React

In the summer of 2020, America was enduring a horrifying COVID-19 pandemic, just like the rest of the world was. People got infected with the virus, millions died, and many more were hospitalized. It was tragic. But something else happened that summer that was tragic.

A number of black men and women were killed by police. Some of the deaths were an accident, but many Americans believe that those accidents were happening too often, and something had to be done. So, starting in June, people began marching on the streets, protesting the murders, and seeking equality for everyone, no matter what their skin color or background. The marches were called "Black Lives Matter." It seemed every major city instantly saw thousands of people peacefully protesting and seeking justice on the streets. That is, except for one city: Nashville.

Six teenagers—Jade Fuller, Nya Collins, Zee Thomas, Kennedy Green, Emma Rose Smith and Mikayla Smith, all high school students, ages fourteen to sixteen—noticed that no one was organizing a march in Nashville. None of these girls knew each other, but each one grew upset at people's silence. The teens wanted to scream...but then realized that wouldn't solve the problem.

Then, they found each other on Twitter and saw what they had in common.

They Never Met Before, but They Had Lots in Common
When each asked why no one was doing something, they began to focus their energy. They said: "Why not us? Why can't students do it?" It took just five days to organize a group they called "Teens4Equality." Their goal was to assemble a peaceful demonstration on June fourth downtown. The teenagers—who come from different backgrounds and attend different high schools—met for the first time on the day of the march. They hoped for as many as a thousand attendees, but then saw that number quickly multiply that day. As they began marching, they collected 15,000 people in Nashville to join them. The girls showed the big difference between "reacting" (just screaming in anger) and "responding" (to solve a problem).

"We felt like we needed to do more because change is not going to just happen overnight," Emma Rose, who is a fifteen-year old sophomore, said in an interview. "We're teens and we weren't seeing any youth speaking up because they didn't feel like they had a voice. We wanted to show teenagers and youth that we need you guys and we do have a voice." When asked what she learned by organizing the protest, Mikayla replied, "No matter what you are or who you are, if you put your mind to it, you can make a difference. A week ago I did not think I would be capable of doing something like this." Their Teens4Equality movement now has over 25,000 followers on social media. It's the power of responding, not reacting.

Think It Over, Talk It Over

1. What was surprising to you about this story of six teens?

2. What helped these students to stay calm and begin to focus on organizing a march?

3. Have you ever wondered why a problem exists? Did you respond instead of react?

To watch a video about this young leader, go to: ICantWaitBook.com

I CAN'T WAIT!

Shamma Al Mazrui

What We Nourish Will Flourish

Shamma Al Mazrui is from the United Arab Emirates. Shamma had dreams for her future as a young girl, but grew up in a part of the world where opportunities for females were often limited. So, she just put one foot in front of the other, accomplished each task she was given by her teachers, and waited to see what would happen.

She probably had no idea what was about to happen to her.

Shamma graduated from New York University, Abu Dhabi, as her nation's first Rhodes Scholar. She got good grades and was involved in lots of activities. Upon graduation, she was then elected as the Minister of State for Youth for her country, when she was only twenty-two years old!

She is the youngest government minister in the world. When she was asked why there aren't more people her age involved as elected officials, she said it's because "people tend to see youth as a problem to solve, not as an asset to leverage." So, older adults set them aside and hope they stay out of trouble, rather than engage them as problem-solvers in their communities. After the election, she assembled a team of young adults who are addressing old problems in new ways and doing well. Her belief is that young people can, indeed, become a problem, if we don't engage them to solve society's problems. They will always find something "interesting" to do, either good or bad.

This Is All About Our Future
Shamma said, "We believe a nation's ability to harness the youth directly impacts... its future. We don't just involve youth, we let them lead. It's baffling how much youth have been sidelined. Too many of us see them as a problem rather than a solution." The key is found in one truth:

"What we nourish will flourish."

Her country created a definition and a report card for youth empowerment. They think youth should be involved in all parts of government. There are six building blocks:

- Voice – Youth should feel they are heard when they speak.
- Recognition – Youth should be affirmed as they achieve goals.
- Purpose – Youth should be offered a meaningful mission.
- Guidance – Youth should be provided with direction.
- Development – Youth should be mentored into maturity.
- Opportunity – Youth should be given chances to succeed.

Think It Over, Talk It Over

1. How would you feel if you were elected to be a leader right after you graduated?
2. What do you think Shamma did to be viewed as someone who was ready to lead?
3. Which of the "building blocks" above do you value most? Do adults offer them to you?

To watch a video about this young leader, go to: ICantWaitBook.com

I CAN'T WAIT!

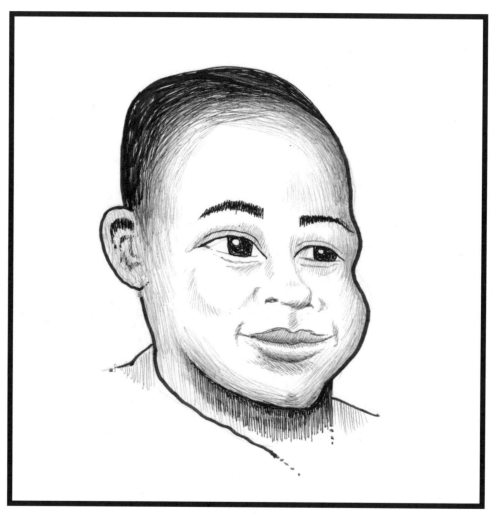

Michael King

I Have a Dream

Michael King grew up in the 1930s and 1940s in Georgia. He was African American, and as a black boy growing up in the South, he saw some of the problems people had between races. In fact, he didn't just see them; he felt them. Often, white people didn't welcome black people into their schools, or sports teams, or restaurants, or even restrooms. It was a very strange time.

So, at fifteen years old, Michael decided he couldn't just stand by and do nothing. In class, he entered a speech contest and wrote a speech about his dream for people of all colors joining hands, and enjoying life together, working, playing, singing, and dining together. It seemed like a logical and realistic dream, but at the time, it was still a dream. It wasn't real for many people of color back then.

Michael felt strongly about equal rights for everyone and used vivid words and images and stories to make his point in the speech. Every one of his classmates listened to him, and they were moved by his words and felt this dream must come true.

The speech was so good, Michael won the contest.

The Boy and the Speech Grew Up

That contest took place in Dublin, Georgia, in 1944. As Michael grew older, he held on to his dream and improved that speech over and over again. When he was in his thirties, Michael gave that speech again. He was an adult and was a leader in the Civil Rights movement during the 1960s in America.

He was getting famous all over the country; he'd been on television and radio, talking about his dream. The speech was given in Detroit, Michigan, and like before, his audience welcomed that speech. People were inspired to work with him toward his dream. Michael even met with the president of the United States and discussed this amazing dream he had. The next year, in August 1963, almost everyone in America heard the speech about his dream.

Michael King had become known as Martin Luther King, Jr. He changed his name to follow in his father's footsteps. On that hot, summer day in Washington, D.C., King was the last speaker to step up and make his short speech. When he finished, he realized that people didn't seem to catch his vision for America. He knew he couldn't stop. One of his friends, Mahalia Jackson, yelled to him from the crowd, "Tell them about your dream, Martin!"

And that's when he began to share that dream he first spoke about at fifteen years old. We now know the speech he gave that day as King's "I Have a Dream" speech. The speech he planned to give was different. But it wasn't enough. King returned to his important thoughts about his dream he had as a teenager. He was just a kid, but he was a kid with some important ideas. And since that time, those ideas have changed the world.

Think It Over, Talk It Over

1. Did you ever have an idea that you felt was very important? What was it?
2. What do you think about the power of words? How did Michael King's words change us?
3. What is one important message you believe you could share with others?

To watch a video about this young leader, go to: ICantWaitBook.com

I CAN'T WAIT!

Viney Kumar

There's an App for That

When Viney Kumar was fifteen and a student at Sydney, Australia's Knox Grammar School, he was visiting Bangalore, India—a city with tons of cars on the road—when he witnessed an everyday sight that distressed him. "I was with my parents in a car, caught in traffic, which was barely moving," he said. "There was this ambulance also stuck in traffic, unable to move. It was noisy and I could barely hear [its] siren until we were really close. I was filled with this helplessness and anger, and I wanted to know why this was happening. I could only imagine who might be inside the ambulance and the fact that they might be battling for their life, and I thought there must be something I could do."

Viney decided to do something back home in Australia.

"So, I went to local hospitals and fire stations and interviewed workers," he says. "They were quite receptive, and this validated my research." It also revealed additional motivational issues. Many drivers either can't hear the siren, or they have a peer-group mentality and will only move over if everyone else is moving, too.

This Kid Got an Idea

Viney discovered that city police already had a system to use smartphones to track trains and buses. So he decided to create an app that could handle vehicle-to-vehicle communication. With GPS technology on a smartphone platform, the app enables people to help save lives and property by cooperating with emergency workers and police.

Viney programmed a solution to help cars get out of the way of ambulances and police ahead of time. He said, "I didn't think I could do it but I wanted to make an attempt. I wanted to have a crack at it."

His invention is nine times more effective than ambulance sirens alone:

- Police can get to a crime faster.
- Ambulances can take patients to the hospital faster.
- Firefighters can reach a house fire faster.

His app is called PART: Police and Ambulance Regulating Traffic. And Viney's idea has already won the praise of others.

Viney Kumar won his age category at the 2013 Google Science Fair, and many city leaders have thanked Viney for his creative thinking. According to the Wharton Global Youth Program, "Viney Kumar's app invention is a great example of how you can think critically about an everyday experience, like approaching ambulance sirens, and add value to it.

Think It Over, Talk It Over

1. Have you ever heard a siren and wondered if the people in trouble would get help in time?
2. Can you name some problems that people just put up with in our everyday life?
3. What product or service that is a regular part of your life would you like to make more effective or efficient? How might you improve upon it?

To watch a video about this young leader, go to: ICantWaitBook.com

I CAN'T WAIT!

Tiger Woods

Balance Your Talents

Anyone who loves golf has heard of Eldrick "Tiger" Woods. When he was just seven months old, his father could tell something was different about his son. Tiger dragged a golf club, a putter, everywhere in his circular baby walker. When he was two, he went on national television and used a golf club tall enough to reach his shoulders to drive a golf ball past an admiring Bob Hope.

Later that year, he entered his first tournament and won the ten-and-under division. By age three, Tiger was learning how to play out of a sand trap. At four, Tiger's dad could drop him off at a golf course at nine in the morning and pick him up eight hours later, sometimes with money in his pocket he'd been given from those foolish enough to doubt his skills.

At age eight, Tiger Woods beat his father in golf for the first time. Dad didn't mind because he was convinced that his son was on his way to become an amazing athlete. By the time Tiger Woods entered Stanford University, he was already quite famous. He was still a teenager but was better than many pro golfers around the world. He became a professional golfer himself when he was only twenty years old. Tiger Woods has been called an overachiever and an early achiever by millions of fans around the world.

But his life was not always wonderful, easy, or fun.

When he was a young boy, he stuttered. He wasn't able to talk very well without stammering through his words. This was not well known until he wrote a letter to a boy who contemplated suicide. Woods wrote, "I know what it's like to be different and to sometimes not fit in. I also stuttered as a child, and I would talk to my dog and he would sit there and listen until he fell asleep. I also took a class for two years to help me, and I finally learned to stop."

In addition, Tiger learned from mistakes he made with his first wife and family. He failed to keep his commitment to his wife and to live by the values his parents had taught him growing up. He later got on television and apologized to his family and to everyone who watched him play. He asked for forgiveness for not setting a good example like he should have done.

Later while driving his car too fast, he was in an accident while he was in California. He hit a tree driving 75 miles an hour and hurt himself badly. He knew it was wrong and was embarrassed by this mistake. In November 2021, he said he would never be a full-time professional golfer again. The good news is—millions got to watch him use his talents as an athlete.

Tiger Woods became an amazing professional golfer. He is tied for first in PGA Tour wins, ranks second in men's major championships, and holds lots of golf records. He's widely regarded as one of the greatest golfers of all time and one of the most famous athletes in modern history.

Think It Over, Talk It Over

1. Have you heard of Tiger Woods? What do you know about him? What do you admire?

2. As a child, Tiger learned to focus on something he was good at. How do we know that?

3. What is something you're good at that you could focus on, grow in, and do as an adult?

To watch a video about this young leader, go to: ICantWaitBook.com

I CAN'T WAIT!

Mary Teresa Bojaxhiu

A Little Saint

It's not very often that a person gets honored with the title of "saint." But that's what happened to Mary Teresa Bojaxhiu, a girl born in Skopje, Albania. At age eighteen, she moved away to Ireland and then to India, which is where she spent most of her life.

When she was still a teenager, she knew she would commit her life to serving people in need. She took a spiritual vow as a young lady to make sacrifices for those who needed help—at first by teaching girls in various schools. She was a wonderful teacher because she loved her students so much and later was asked to become the leader (headmistress) of a school in Calcutta.

While she served in one school, however, she felt an inward "calling within a calling." She knew she wanted to serve people in need, but as she looked out the windows of the school, she saw people living in deep poverty. They had little to eat or to wear and would often die of starvation.

Eventually, she had to do something more than watch them from the window and pray.

She later left her position as an educator to serve those poor people. Along the way, she learned five different languages so she could communicate with local people, and she learned the customs of those people so she could relate to them well.

No sacrifice was too great for her to make people feel loved and to provide for them. She gave her life to those who had nothing. Her main goal was to take care of them until they died and to make sure they felt loved when they died.

- She would hold babies in her arms to make sure they felt loved.
- She would clean the sores on the legs of those who had leprosy.
- She would hug and encourage those who were lonely on the streets.
- She would help those who had tuberculosis and had little time to live.

When someone asked Teresa to describe her job, she smiled and simply said:
"I am a little pencil in the hands of a writing God who is sending a love letter to the world."

As she matured, she was no longer called "Sister Teresa" but "Mother Teresa" as she built a charity that cared for the sick and the poor. Teresa never tried to become famous, but over her lifetime, as people learned about what she was doing, she was voted as one of the most admired and influential women in the world. In 1979, she won a Nobel Peace Prize.

She had started the largest order of its kind, The Sisters of Charity. Several other charities followed in her footsteps and by 2012, her mission had 4,500 nuns serving in 133 nations. Even though Mother Teresa died in 1997, her legacy lives on and continues to this day, with people like her loving and serving others, one person at a time.

Think It Over, Talk It Over

1. How do you think Teresa discovered what she wanted to do with her life at such a young age?
2. What do you admire most about her story?
3. Have you ever felt the urge to serve someone else who didn't have much? Did you do it?

To watch a video about this young leader, go to: ICantWaitBook.com

I CAN'T WAIT!

Wolfgang Amadeus Mozart

The Music Was in Him

If you know anything about music history, you've heard the name: Mozart. He was born on January 27, 1756. He lived during the same period as George Washington and Ben Franklin, but he lived in Austria, not America. He is widely known as one of the greatest composers of all time. He only lived about thirty-six years, but he sure crammed a lot of his creativity into those short years. Unlike any other composer in musical history, he wrote in all the musical genres (styles) of his day and excelled in every one of them.

So how did he influence the world of music so much in such a short life? Believe it or not, Mozart composed his first piece of music in 1761, when he was only five years old. Think about it—by kindergarten, he was already creating songs. One reason he learned to do this so fast was listening to his older sister and to his dad, who both played musical instruments. By age six, he had performed before two imperial courts. In 1763, Mozart and his sister, Maria Anna, went on tour. For three years the siblings toured western Europe, performing in major cities such as Munich, Augsburg, Paris, and London. The boy was only seven years of age.

Most people remember Mozart for his symphonies. He was an amazing composer of musical symphonies. This is a very difficult thing to do because this form of music involves several instruments. How could he do this?

One reason is, he got his start early on. He composed his first symphony when he was eight years old. Because he was so young, historians believe his father likely transcribed the song.

His dad realized how gifted his son was and really supported him in his musical goals. His dad was proud that his son was more talented than he was—and he worked to help Mozart to succeed.

The boy composed his first opera at age twelve.

What Made Mozart So Special?
Mozart was like many kids today. He was very talented, and he combined his gift for learning and performing with his love of music and of animals. Many of his early songs were about animals, including his own dog, named Bimberl.

These two themes were his inspiration. When we think about what we can learn from his life, these three examples rise to the top:

1. He started as a kid and didn't wait till he was older to use his talents.
2. He was hungry to keep learning and trying new types of music as he grew.
3. He and his sister practiced a lot, for hours each day.

These realities enabled Mozart to be so successful at such a young age. Today, it's quite common for people to live until they are eighty or ninety years old. Mozart only lived until he was barely thirty-six. But because he was willing to work hard and practice for long hours, he was able to write over six hundred songs in his short life.

Today, symphonies around the world still perform his music.

Think It Over, Talk It Over

1. Mozart watched his dad and sister play music as a kid. How did that influence him?
2. Can you think of anything you love and are good at that you could practice for long hours?
3. What's the greatest lesson you can learn from the life of Mozart?

To watch a video about this young leader, go to: ICantWaitBook.com

I CAN'T WAIT!

The Girls of Iran

Freedom Isn't Free

If you live in America and have never traveled to other parts of the world, you may be surprised to see how different other nations are. In some countries, girls have far less rights than guys.

In the country of Iran, women have fewer rights than many other countries do. For example:

- Females have restricted voting rights.
- Women's rights are restricted in terms of their choice for marriage or divorce.
- Divorced women's rights are restricted compared to men in child custody.
- Girls are even restricted from attending a soccer game.
- Married women can't travel out of the country without their husband's permission.
- Females have even been sent to jail for speaking out on behalf of women's rights.

Even though President Hassan Rouhani said he wants to see reform happen, much of Iran's power still lies in their supreme ruler, Ayatollah Ali Khamenei. He is a traditional Muslim leader who believes rights should stay limited for ladies. While some women don't mind at all, many don't like that they're forced to wear certain clothing, including a headscarf called the hijab. Under Iran's strict interpretation of Islam since 1979, girls over the age of nine are required to cover their heads and everything but the face and hands. Offenders face fines or jail time. But in every society, it is often the youth who take a stand and oppose the status quo.

One Young Lady Named Atefeh
One young lady named Atefeh Ahmadi started seeing posts on Facebook, showing videos of females standing on electrical boxes or walls in the public square and removing their head scarves. So, one day, she tried it herself and her video and pictures went viral on social media. On March eighth, International Women's Day, she tried a new kind of protest. She said, "Me and two of my friends went to the subway. We sat in the 'women only' car and sang a well-known song (about the power of women). We also handed out pamphlets promoting women's rights."

The song drew attention, and after she was identified in a documentary as one of the participants, she chose to leave Iran for Turkey later that month. Yet the protests continued and spread to other issues beyond the headscarf. Later, Facebook and Twitter were banned in the Islamic Republic, but many girls and young women in that area access these social media sites through private online networks that hide the user's locations. They are slowly making a difference.

By late 2017, the police said they would stop arresting people for dress code violations. The girls know that change will not happen overnight, but over time.

Think It Over, Talk It Over

1. Have you ever seen someone's rights violated? Did it seem unfair? How did you feel?
2. Did you ever take a stand for your rights or gain justice for someone else?
3. What's the greatest lesson you can learn from these young ladies from Iran?

To watch a video about this young leader, go to: ICantWaitBook.com

The Girls of Iran

I CAN'T WAIT!

Liam Elkind

Turning a Bad Day Around

Liam was a Yale University sophomore who returned home when the "shelter in place" order was given on campus in 2020. The pandemic hit everyone. While quarantined at home, he knew he'd have a lot of time on his hands and no parties to attend. He was getting bored and frustrated at his situation. His parents saw him pondering how to process this strange season and suggested he could help Carolyn. She was an 85-year-old shut-in who had no good way to get food on a regular basis.

Liam decided to take groceries to Carolyn and offer her a virtual hug and some friendly conversation. After taking food to this elderly woman, he wondered how many other people in the area needed the same kind of help. When he discovered the need was considerable, he began an outreach called Invisible Hands. They recruited 3,500 volunteers to deliver food to those who needed it. Everyone won. What a way to use a pandemic.

Students who had time and energy got a chance to serve those in need. People who desperately needed help got their needs met. A community got a big problem solved.

Liam is part of a growing population of students who embrace social entrepreneurship.

Social entrepreneurship—born out of the cooperative movement that began in nineteenth-century Europe—gained traction in the 1980s and 1990s with the emergence of social innovation and social enterprise schools of thought and practice.

Social entrepreneurship is defined as entrepreneurial activity undertaken with the explicit objective of addressing societal problems. It is this convergence that informs the unique hybrid nature of social enterprises.

The fact is, in 2005, studies revealed that more teens volunteered than adults. According to a report issued by the Corporation for National and Community Service, 55 percent of American teenagers volunteered that year, compared to only 29 percent of adults. Among its findings, the report found that the likelihood of a young person volunteering is directly related to his or her connections to social institutions such as family, church or religious group, and school. Nearly three-quarters of all youth who volunteer do so at least in part through religious organizations, school-based groups, or leadership groups such as scouts or 4H.

The good news?

Only 5 percent of teens attributed their volunteer activities to a mandatory school requirement.

Liam is one example of a student who took an interruption and made it an introduction to a whole new way of getting things done.

Think It Over, Talk It Over

1. What impresses you the most about Liam's story?
2. Have you ever experienced a problem and wanted to help others who had that problem?
3. Did you ever step out to help someone who struggled? What happened?

To watch a video about this young leader, go to: ICantWaitBook.com

I CAN'T WAIT!

Norris Guidry

Getting Caught by the Police

A boy named Norris began mowing lawns a few years ago. I'm not talking about mowing his own lawn; he was doing that already. I mean, he began mowing lawns for other people who needed it, starting with a disabled neighbor who lived nearby. He didn't make a big deal of it. He just marched over and mowed their lawn. And he's continued since that time. Norris now mows many lawns—for free—just because he knows it's easier for him to do it than it is for others.

Today, Norris hopes to turn this into a business soon.

People have taken notice of this teen. Frozen Rayne SnoCones began giving police officers "tickets" to offer any kid they spot doing something good for someone else. One officer spotted Norris and gave him one for a free snow cone. They call it a "Caught You" ticket. Over time, Norris began providing lawn care for the elderly, disabled, single moms, and veterans. The result? Let's just say Norris has enjoyed his fair share of snow cones. Police "caught" him!

But that's not why he's doing the lawn care.

Norris would tell you he simply matched a skill he had with a passion he had to help those in need. Mowing lawns came to mind. So, instead of waiting or analyzing whether it was a good idea or not, he just acted on his passion. His aspiration to serve gave him inspiration to act.

The Key Is to Get Started

When I was young, I began to notice this connection between my inspiration and my aspirations. Once I had a goal, I instantly felt inspired to go to work.

Want to find what you should do?

First, ask yourself what makes you sad or angry. Often, a calling begins with a negative emotion about something that must be done. Talk about any interests you have in something important.

Next, remember: your passions are not random. Think about Norris, the grass cutter. What does his passion for mowing lawns say about him? What could you do about your passion?

Third, consider your past experiences. They inform our desires. I know a 91-year old man who was bullied as a kid and two boys helped him. Today, he's that person for others who feel alone.

Finally, take one first step. It doesn't need to be amazing. The longer you wait, the easier it is to wait longer. There will always be excuses. Get started now. I learned long ago…

- I don't need a better computer to become a writer.
- I don't need a better guitar to become a musician.
- I don't need a better camera to become a photographer.
- What I need…is to get started.

Think It Over, Talk It Over

1. Have you ever done something like Norris did? You saw a need and you acted on it?
2. What keeps you from getting started when you get a good idea?
3. Do you have any passions you could do something about today or tomorrow?

To watch a video about this young leader, go to: ICantWaitBook.com

I CAN'T WAIT!

Michelle Kunimoto

Finding Planets While Stargazing

A young lady named Michelle Kunimoto did something very, very unusual. She discovered something even professional scientists have never discovered. It seemed like her whole life was destined to be a little special. Michelle grew up in Canada and has always loved science. While attending high school, she grew interested in astronomy. She described it this way: "I became certain I wanted to study astronomy after my dad introduced my brother and me to Star Trek: The Original Series back in high school."

Do you know the characters from that original TV show—Captain Kirk, Mr. Spock, and Dr. "Bones" McCoy? The theme of this show rings in the ears of anyone who watched it: "To boldly go where no man has gone before."

In a way, that's what Michelle did as a student.

Once she graduated from high school, she decided to study astronomy in college. Then, she went on to get her post-graduate degree (PhD) at the University of British Columbia. It was while she was there that she made this incredible discovery.

By combing through data collected by NASA's planet-hunting Kepler telescope, she patiently observed all kinds of shapes and lights. She made notes as she waited and observed.

After hours and even weeks of work, Michelle discovered evidence of seventeen new planets, including one that is the same shape as the Earth and seems to be in a habitable zone.

It Took a Lot of Patience
Michelle had to study 20,000 stars before she found seventeen that may have planets orbiting them. That took lots of work and lots of patience. Finding them was like finding a needle-in-a-haystack, which is why other NASA researchers may have missed them. Michelle explained that "every time a planet passes in front of a star, it blocks a part of that star's light and causes a temporary decrease in the star's brightness. By finding these dips…you can start to piece together information about the planet, such as its size and how long it takes to orbit its sun."

As mentioned, one of the planets she found appears to be more like the Earth and in the "habitable zone" of its star. But Michelle explained, "This planet is about a thousand light years away, so we're not getting there anytime soon!" Then she added, "But this is a really exciting find!"

No student has ever discovered this many planets—which illustrates that sometimes new discoveries require young eyes and a fresh approach to get the job done.

Think It Over, Talk It Over

1. What do you think is amazing about Michelle's story?
2. Have you ever done something as a kid that even adults haven't done?
3. What fascinates you that makes you want to study it and do something new?

To watch a video about this young leader, go to: ICantWaitBook.com

I CAN'T WAIT!

Denis Estimon

No One Eats Alone

Denis Estimon does not claim to be anyone special. Yet, when he was a high school student just a few years ago, he did something very special.

Denis attended Boca High School in Boca Raton, Florida. Even though the school has 3,400 students attending, many of them are lonely. (It is possible to feel lonely even when you're not alone.) At lunch time, everyone splits into their social groups, but not everyone gets included. Some teens are marginalized. Some have no group to eat with. So—they eat alone.

Denis Estimon realized, "It's not a good feeling to be alone. I don't want anyone to feel that." Denis himself understands that feeling. He is a Haitian immigrant who came to America when he was in the first grade. He remembers not knowing anyone at school. He remembers feeling isolated, especially at lunch. Now, he's popular and has lots of friends, but he's never forgotten that early feeling of loneliness.

In fact, he discovered there's a loneliness problem across our country. Millions of students suffer from loneliness even more than they do from anxiety. It's the number one challenge among teens. So, along with some friends, Denis started a club called We Dine Together. Students in this club meet at the beginning of lunch period, then go out to make sure no one is "starving" for friendship at lunch.

When they see someone sitting alone, they'll sit next to them and ask how they're doing; they'll find out if the person wants to be alone or if they'd like some company.

Most appreciate a new friend who initiates conversation. For new kids, this club is a godsend. Since the first year, hundreds of friendships were born.

Imagine what it feels like if you're new and alone and some of the coolest kids in school come up and want to spend time with you. One student athlete from the football team even quit the team so he could spend more time with the club, meeting new people. He said, "I don't mind giving up a football scholarship. This is what I want to do with my time."

So many students who understood what it felt like to be alone have joined and now offer a little friendship and a listening ear to someone else who feels alone today. Since beginning We Dine Together, Denis has graduated from high school but not from this goal. He now travels, starting new clubs all over the country; he's started hundreds of chapters all over the U.S.

Each We Dine Together family is led by a Be Strong Student State Representative, leading change in four key areas: Resilience Training, Acts of Kindness, Advocacy and Awareness, all while maintaining their mission: "no one eats alone."

Change can start with one person.

Think It Over, Talk It Over

1. Think about Denis's story. What do you think motivated him to start the club?
2. Have you ever experienced a problem and wanted to help others who had that problem?
3. Did you ever step out to help someone who struggled? What happened?

To watch a video about this young leader, go to: ICantWaitBook.com

I CAN'T WAIT!

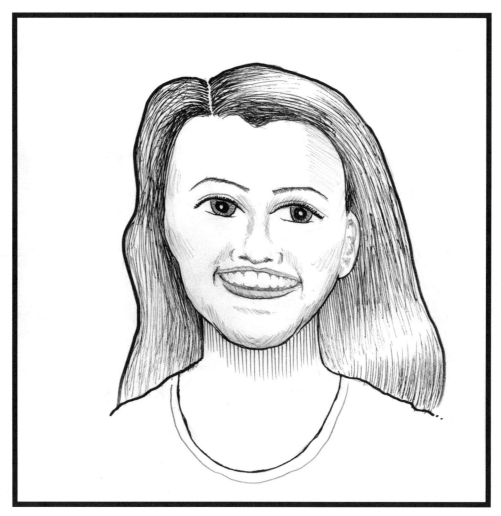

Amy Waldroop

Amy's Big Decision

Sometimes, families are broken. It can happen for lots of reasons, but believe it or not, in some families, the parents are not able to lead their children well. In the Waldroop family, Amy's dad was gone, and her mom was addicted to drugs. These drugs often left her mom either unable to function or completely unconscious. This left the responsibility of raising young children up to Amy, who was a child herself. That she was able to do so was a sort of miracle.

In fact, Amy's whole life was a miracle.

She was born dead. She was the smaller of a set of twins and wasn't breathing when her drug-addicted mom, Jan, gave birth to her. The doctors struggled to save her life, and Amy's life was a struggle ever since. Without her parents around to lead the family, Amy began leading at a young age. Since childhood, Amy took care of her younger siblings.

First it was her sister Amanda, four years younger than her. Then, when Amy was ten, along came Adam, followed by Joseph, and then Anthony. As a young girl, Amy had to feed and change the babies, put them to sleep when they cried, and care for them when they were sick. It was so much sometimes, Amy cried and felt she just couldn't do it. The truth is, Amy had to act like an adult when she was a kid because her parents were not able to act like adults. It was so sad, and yet Amy rose to the challenge.

When This Story Became Known
Trouble came when this family's lifestyle became known at their school. Jan would forget to sign her kids up for the lunch program, so they sat in the lunchroom, hungry. They would get sick and often, Amy would go to the drugstore and not even know what to ask for from the pharmacist. Finally, Amy told a social worker what was happening. When the worker asked why she didn't say something sooner, Amy replied: "Because I thought we'd all be taken away to different places."

That's exactly what happened. When her mother, Jan, went to prison, no one could find a family to take all of the children. The judge ruled they would have to split up and go to different families. By then, Amy was a teenager and old enough to make some big decisions. And that's exactly what she did. She chose to defend her right to take care of her brothers and sister, even though she was just nineteen years old. It took some debate, but Amy won her case. As a teen, she became the official leader of her own family—which were her siblings.

As the story became known, wonderful things began to happen. The magazine, Reader's Digest, chose to tell her story and raised money to help Amy and her family. Her story later became a Lifetime movie, where producers adapted the tale and called it: "Gracie's Choice."

Think It Over, Talk It Over

1. What do you believe motivated Amy to care for her siblings?
2. Have you ever had to take on a job that you felt was an "adult responsibility"?
3. Did you ever do something important and felt overwhelmed? What happened?

To watch a video about this young leader, go to: ICantWaitBook.com

I CAN'T WAIT!

Evan Spiegel

When Homework Pays

Did you ever dream that a homework assignment could turn into a job for you? How about a career? That's exactly what happened to Evan Spiegel as a college student at Stanford University. In fact, his idea was so surprising that he decided to give his full attention to building a business and never turned back. He turned his homework assignment into a billion-dollar empire.

Here is how it all started.

After graduating high school, Evan was accepted at Stanford University. It was in his fraternity that he met Bobby Murphy, who soon became a friend and later his business partner. Evan was a Product Design major, since he was interested in creating technology products that people could use to make their life better.

According to Stanford's Alumni Spotlight, "In 2011, during Spiegel's junior year, he stood up in a Stanford product design class to present an idea for his final project. It would be a mobile app, he explained, where friends could share photos that would disappear—forever—in a matter of seconds. Everyone said, 'That is a terrible idea,' Spiegel remembered. 'Nobody is going to use it,' they said." In fact, fellow students told him the only people who would use it would be kids who want to use it for the wrong reasons.

But Evan felt he was on to something. He knew he had a good idea.

Later that year, Evan Spiegel went to work on his concept with classmates at Stanford. They originally called this app, "Picaboo." It was a prototype of his product. As you might guess, they later changed the name to Snapchat. The app grew popular almost instantly. By the end of 2012, Evan had dropped out of college to work on his app, which had already reached one million daily active users. It's only gotten bigger since then.

Today, it's amazing to consider that it all started with a student and an idea.

Stanford University summarizes the story this way: "Evan Spiegel became the co-founder of Snapchat, the popular social media app that allows users to send messages that disappear shortly after being opened. Each day, hundreds of millions of people use Snapchat to send disappearing photos and video clips.

Interested in technology from a young age, Spiegel continues his passion today as Chief Executive Officer of Snapchat. In 2018, he returned to Stanford to finish his college degree and since then has donated millions of dollars to the school and to other charities. In 2014, Spiegel was named as one of TIME Magazine's 100 Most Influential People in the World."

Think It Over, Talk It Over

1. What's the most interesting part of Evan's story to you?
2. Did you ever have an idea that you felt was good, but other people didn't understand it?
3. What is the biggest lesson we can learn from Evan's story?

To watch a video about this young leader, go to: ICantWaitBook.com

I CAN'T WAIT!

Albert Einstein

Learning to Teach Yourself

Anyone who's taken a science class probably knows the name, Albert Einstein. Millions remember him as the scientist who changed our way of thinking about time and space.

But did you know his childhood was rough?

Albert Einstein was considered a slow learner when he was young. Growing up in Germany, he struggled with learning to speak, and with learning to write in English. Once he did learn to speak, he often just mumbled to himself. His slow development caused him to be curious about other subjects—topics that most of us overlook—like time and space.

Like most of us, Albert was weak in some subjects but strong in others. Some people claim that Einstein failed math when he was young, but this is not true. Einstein himself said that he excelled in mathematics and that his parents encouraged him by purchasing him advanced math textbooks for him to learn the proofs on his own.

By the age of twelve, he taught himself geometry. At the age of fifteen, Albert quit high school, disgusted by boring lessons and strict teachers. He followed his family to Italy, where they had moved their failing business. After six months of wandering and loafing, he attended a Swiss school. At the age of sixteen, he failed an exam in order to qualify to train as an electrical engineer. At this point, he chose a new plan for his future.

Einstein decided to focus on math and physics so he could become a teacher. It was at this point, he had a breakthrough and probably didn't even know it.

His Breakthrough as a Teen

Albert Einstein wrote his first scientific essay in the summer of 1895. He was only sixteen years old. This essay became the foundation upon which he totally changed our approach to physics.

By this time, young Albert recognized he was different from his fellow students. He did not assume he was special, just different. Some things in his life were a struggle, while others were easy. In 1905, after graduating from college, he struggled to get a teaching job or get a doctoral dissertation accepted. So, he began working six days a week in a Swiss patent office. It was during this time that he wrote four papers that completely changed physics. The most notable paper was on his equation: $E=mc^2$. His theory of relativity transformed how scientists in our day understood time and space.

People began listening to him more and more and eventually, Albert Einstein led the way in redefining nuclear physics.

The famous physicist won a Nobel Peace Prize that same year by explaining the science behind today's solar energy revolution. He was twenty-six.

Think It Over, Talk It Over

1. Did you learn anything new about Albert Einstein's story?
2. Did you know he struggled with some subjects, which led him to focus on others?
3. What is the biggest lesson we can learn from Albert's story?

To watch a video about this young leader, go to: ICantWaitBook.com

I CAN'T WAIT!

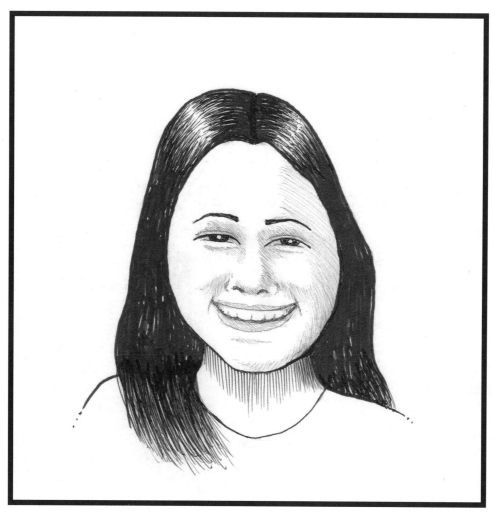

Karly Hou

Students Helping Students

You probably remember when everyone around the world was asked to quarantine during the COVID-19 pandemic in 2020. The pandemic changed the way schools taught classes for two years and during that time, many students struggled to stay engaged while at home. But did you know his childhood was rough?

That first year, when classes were shut down and turned into online courses, a group of California college students spotted a need in younger students. Karly Hou was a sophomore at Harvard University who came home to Palo Alto to finish the year virtually. That's when she realized she had to do something to help the many students who were having trouble.

With extra time on her hands, Karly and some friends from different colleges decided to start an online teaching center called Wave Learning Festival. It's all about taking a bunch of college students who love certain subjects and using their knowledge to teach younger students in a way that is fun and engaging.

That way, the young kids don't lose what they learned earlier, and can continue learning from other students who are a little older than they are. Over a few months, more and more college students volunteered to teach these free, live interactive classes. They taught everything from science to athletics to filmmaking.

Wave Learning Festival launched in June 2020 and within a month, it had over three thousand students from thirty-one different countries logged on to learn.

Eventually, they grew to ten thousand kids.

Can Students Really Help Students?
Karly described what happened this way: "We built this really awesome community of learners and none of these students are here because they have to be. There are no grades and no tests."

The learners think it's amazing too.

Ana Rodrigues, who was a senior in high school, saw a friend post a link to the Wave Learning Festival on Instagram. "The minute I saw it I immediately thought, 'wow, free learning! This is awesome," she said. Ana signed up for three art history courses that year. What's really amazing is Ana's story is just one of thousands of other stories like this.

I love the fact that Karly and her friends didn't wait for someone else to solve the problem. They didn't expect an adult to solve it for them. And they didn't complain about the problem, but instead did something about it that was within their power. The college students simply chose a subject that they loved and were good at explaining.

Then, they started a website that enabled younger teens to find them and let them know where they needed help. As they got connected, the magic began. Students helped students, and later they got special speakers involved. In the end, everyone won—the teachers and the learners. What a great way to get through a tough time.

Think It Over, Talk It Over

1. What do you like most about Karly's simple idea?
2. Have you ever taught a younger kid something that you knew well?
3. What is the best lesson from Karly's story? What can we learn from her?

To watch a video about this young leader, go to: ICantWaitBook.com

I CAN'T WAIT!

Steve Jobs

How Do You Like Them Apples?

Do you have a laptop computer, a tablet, or a smartphone? If you do, you'll be interested to know that a young guy named Steve Jobs played a big role in the growth of computer technology. He got started as a teenager, working at Atari Corporation, as a videogame designer. It was then that he became fascinated with technology.

After trying college in Oregon, he returned to Silicon Valley, California, in 1974 and reconnected with a high school friend named Stephen Wozniak, who was working for the Hewlett-Packard Company. On the side, Stephen was designing his own computer logic board. Both of them felt these machines were going to be important to people in the future. When the two showed it to Hewlett-Packard, the idea got rejected. That's when Steve Jobs and Steve Wozniak decided to start a business and create their own personal computer.

Steve Jobs was only 21 years old—not even old enough to graduate from college.

The Apple I, as they called the logic board, was built in Steve Jobs' family garage with money they earned by selling Jobs' Volkswagen minibus and Wozniak's expensive calculator. To make sure their new computer didn't look like it was some science fair project, they added a keyboard, which sort of looked like a typewriter. Then, they molded a plastic case as the outside cover. It looked cool and very modern.

The Apple Company
Steve Jobs knew he was going to revolutionize computer technology, much like Isaac Newton revolutionized science and math.

Remembering how Newton saw an apple fall from a tree, which enabled him to discover the law of gravity, Steve Jobs chose the name Apple for his company. To ensure their logo didn't look like a strawberry, they designed it with a bite taken out of the apple. They also decided to call their computers Macintosh, or "Mac," which is a type of apple.

Steve called his team of computer designers "artists," since he wanted his products to look like works of art. He actually helped to start other companies too, including a tech company called NeXT and an animation company called Pixar. Ever heard of that one? Years ago, Steve Jobs and Bob Iger agreed to allow Disney to buy Pixar and lead all the work in their animation studios.

Why? Because the team that Steve Jobs put together could be described as:

- Pioneers – People who go first and start new things we never saw before.
- Innovators – People who take existing products or ideas and improve them.

It's amazing to think that these amazing pieces of smart technology began with a teenager who was different from everyone else and who insisted on doing things differently and excellently.

Think It Over, Talk It Over

1. What do you think is the biggest difference between Steve Jobs and other inventors?
2. In what ways are you different from other kids your age?
3. What can we learn from Steve Jobs that we can apply in our lives?

To watch a video about this young leader, go to: ICantWaitBook.com

I CAN'T WAIT!

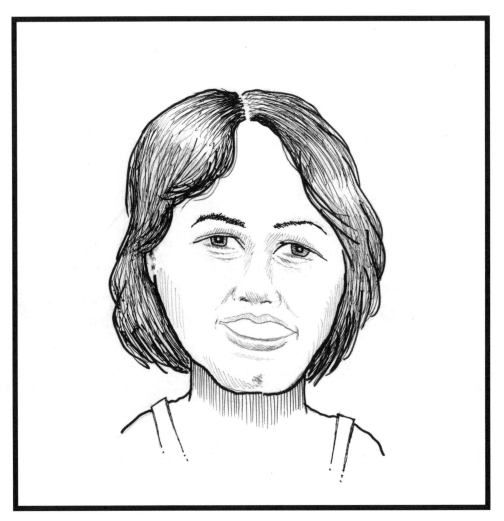

Tammy Hendley

A Small Step That Made a Big Difference

Sometimes a small action can make a huge difference. Just ask Tammy Hendley. Tammy was fourteen years old when she was skimming through a Reader's Digest magazine. In it, there was an article titled "Missing: 100,000 Children a Year." It was about how many kids run away or disappear each year in America, and many are never found again. The magazine showed photographs of several of those kids, and Tammy began staring at one of them. She felt she recognized one of those kids.

The picture looked like another Tammy she knew. Tammy Ann Pickerman was a teen who worked alongside her mother as a nurse's aide. Tammy showed the picture to her mom, and both agreed—the photo looked a lot like the Pickerman girl. At that point, Tammy Hendley worried about what to do.

Even though the picture resembled the girl she thought she knew, what if she was wrong? Would she get the hopes up of the Pickerman family, only to let them down if she was mistaken? The picture listed the missing teen as Marian Wavie Batson, who had been living in Florida and was now aged sixteen. She had been missing since January 7, 1980, which was two and a half years earlier.

So much of this story could be wrong, but Tammy felt she had to do something.

So, she asked her aunt Liddy to call the number listed in the magazine. They quickly discovered someone else had spotted Marian Wavie Batson (the girl they knew as Tammy Pickerman) and said she worked as a waitress at a truck stop in Florida.

After several failed attempts to track her down, the Pinkermans finally got a clue as to where she was.

She had run away from home and moved from Georgia to Florida. Even though she was young, she had fallen in love with a man and gotten a job hundreds of miles away. It was in Florida that Tammy's parents found their daughter. She was far away from home and had been missing for two and a half years.

They hugged and cried, so happy to be together again. The parents found notes Tammy had written to them. One of them said: "I love and miss you more than I could ever explain. I'm ashamed of what I've done. I pray every night that God will send you my love and take care of you so that one day I'll see all of you again. I want you to know how really sorry I am…"

The Amazing Part of This Story
What I love most about this story is that it was a teenager who helped to find another teenager. Tammy Hendley could have seen the picture and decided it was easier to not get involved. In fact, she could have overlooked the photograph completely. It's easier to sit and do nothing than to get up and act on what you believe to be right. But Tammy is a leader:

- Leaders notice realities that others may not see.
- Leaders spot details when others miss them.
- Leaders are observant and identify things that need to change.

Think It Over, Talk It Over

1. Have you ever felt it was right to do something and decided not to act on it?
2. What makes it hard to display the courage to act on something uncertain?
3. How does Tammy Hendley's story make you feel? Why?

To watch a video about this young leader, go to: ICantWaitBook.com

I CAN'T WAIT!

Mark Zuckerberg

Screenager

Even while Mark Zuckerberg was still a student, many people had already heard of him. He is the person who is known for creating Facebook, the social networking website that now has nearly three billion monthly users around the world.

He got started very early.

Mark always loved computers. In fact, he learned the BASIC programming language at a nearby college, and at the age of twelve, he developed an instant-messaging application that his father used in his office. He just had a knack for technology, and he saw it as a way that people could get to know each other better. When he and his three friends created Facebook, they hoped they would enable students to meet each other—especially guys and girls. When it first launched, Facebook was just for Harvard students. Then, it was for Ivy League college students. Later, it was for any university student. Later, it became available to high schoolers, anywhere. Finally, it became available to anyone thirteen and older.

So, why did Mark and his friends pick the name?

A "face book" is a student directory featuring photos and basic information. For years, they were printed booklets. Today, we have the opportunity to enjoy meeting people on a screen, digitally.

So, Mark felt it was a new way to have access to a "face book" and he called theirs: The Facebook. Mark dropped out of Harvard University his sophomore year to give Facebook his full attention.

Not Perfect But Better
Mark certainly isn't perfect. His smarts didn't prevent him from hurting the feelings of the three friends with whom he started Facebook, and they filed a lawsuit against him for stealing ideas. The attorneys and court system were able to work out a compromise and solve the problem. Sometimes, being smart doesn't mean you're smart in all areas—like relationships. In addition, his platform, Facebook, isn't perfect, requiring his team to constantly work on making it better.

The good news is, Mark is an example of a teen who found a way to improve upon a current idea and make it far better than what people had seen up to that point. When we examine Mark Zuckerberg's life, it seems he lives by these principles:

- Always look to make things better.
- Teach yourself what you need to know.
- Don't wait till later; start now.

Mark Zuckerberg launched Facebook from his dorm room at Harvard University at age nineteen. Still a teenager. Still a student. But he couldn't wait to change the world.

Think It Over, Talk It Over

1. What part of Mark's story is most amazing to you?
2. How do you think Mark handled being so famous at such a young age?
3. Did you ever have an idea but felt you needed to wait to get started? What did you do?

To watch a video about this young leader, go to: ICantWaitBook.com

I CAN'T WAIT!

Shubham Banerjee

A Vision for the Blind

Can you imagine what it would be like to be blind? You wouldn't be able to read this book, at least not unless you had a Braille version of it. Back in the nineteenth century, Louis Braille invented a system for blind people to read, when he was fifteen years old. It was another teenager, Shubham Banerjee, who saw a need today and created a solution for it—when he was only twelve years old.

According to the National Federation of the Blind, fewer than ten percent of the 1.3 million blind Americans can read Braille. When you compare that to the past, it's awful. In the 1950s, more than half of blind children learned to read books with the Braille system.

So, what did Shubham do?

This twelve-year-old kid was looking for a good idea for a project for the 2014 science fair. He stumbled across these facts about blind kids today and how so few have access to books and reading, since so much information has moved to voice-activated devices. Shubham found out that millions of blind kids cannot afford a voice-to-text device. He then thought: What if he could reduce the cost of a Braille printer from two thousand dollars to two hundred? That would be fantastic, but some Silicon Valley start-up companies had been trying to achieve this, with little success.

I guess it took a smart kid who believed it could be done.

His Problem Got Bigger and More Important

Shubham's original problem was to find a good science project for school, but his problem actually became far more important in his mind—he actually wanted to create something for people in need. He took several weeks and seven attempts to get his project done, but he finally built a prototype (a first kind of machine) using Lego Mindstorms EV3 robotics kit and some small electrical components that cost a few dollars. They were able to print the six "dots" of the Braille system and enable someone who is blind to read.

At thirteen years old, Shubham was a Santa Clara, California, high school freshman and the inventor of Braigo, a groundbreaking low-cost Braille printer-embosser. The Braigo printer is a small, portable machine that looks a lot like any other printer—only it spits out strings of raised bumps instead of flat text on a page.

Shubham Banerjee co-founded a small company, Braigo Labs, to help further develop the printer for educational and home use, as well as provide information to anyone who wants to buy the Mindstorms kit and try making a Braigo v1.0 at home. How did he come up with the name: Braigo? Well, it's a combination of "Braille" and "Lego," which is the reading system and the name of the kit his parents got for him to build the machine.

What I love most about this story is: this teen wasn't blind. He could see just fine. His inspiration was simply to solve a problem for people who are blind, even when he didn't know any of them. Shubham loves solving problems.

Think It Over, Talk It Over

1. Does it feel like a kid who's twelve is too young to do something this big? Why? Why not?
2. Why do you think this young teen got so inspired to help blind people read?
3. Did you ever see someone with a problem and felt you should help solve it? Did you do something about it?

To watch a video about this young leader, go to: ICantWaitBook.com

I CAN'T WAIT!

Steven Spielberg

Use What You Have

Many people believe that Steven Spielberg is the most successful Hollywood director of all time. He loved making movies, even as a kid in the 1960s. In fact, he made his first movie, Escape to Nowhere at age 13, with a cast made up of school classmates. It was a forty-minute war film that sparked his interest to make more films. He had a blast.

Steven was born in Cincinnati, Ohio, and later grew up in a typical suburban childhood in Arizona and California. He got his start making backyard Super 8-millimeter short films, which was how people shot films back then. No one had video cameras or high-tech equipment until years later. These cameras were a relatively cheap way to make home movies as a hobby. But Steven did it as more than a hobby. Movie making would become his passion.

In 1964, at the age of seventeen, Spielberg wrote, directed, and edited a 135-minute science-fiction film entitled Firelight, elements of which would later end up in his 1977 sci-fi epic, Close Encounters of The Third Kind, whose twenty million dollar budget is a lot more than Firelight's five hundred dollar budget. Most of the money needed to make Firelight was raised through friends and family, the cast came from Spielberg's school, Arcadia High School, his sister Nancy played a major part in it, and Steven composed the score himself on a clarinet. His mother created the sheet music for it, and it was performed by the high school marching band. Not bad for a teenager.

This Film Was Just the Beginning
The movie was screened only once, at a local theater, for an audience of five hundred people. Spielberg counted the profits that night and later said, "We charged a dollar a ticket. Five hundred people came to the movie, and I think somebody probably paid two dollars, because we made a one dollar profit that night, and that was it." So, a five hundred dollar film was watched by five hundred people and ended up making $501. Coincidence? Probably so. But Steven began to make money from his projects from that point on. For Steven and movies—it was love at first sight.

Back then, there was very little written about how to make or direct a film. Steven had to figure it out on his own. When he applied to a major film school, the University of Southern California, he was rejected twice. Steven, however, did not give up. He kept teaching himself as he attended Brookdale Community College, then California State University at Long Beach. It all turned into a groundbreaking career. So—what are the lessons Steven teaches us about succeeding?

- Start small.
- Use what you have.
- Stay focused.
- Don't give up.

Think It Over, Talk It Over

1. Have you seen any of Steven Spielberg's movies? Look some up to find out.
2. What is most impressive to you about his story?
3. Did you ever take on a project and have to work very hard to finish it? When?

To watch a video about this young leader, go to: ICantWaitBook.com

I CAN'T WAIT!

"Mo" Bridges

Mo's Bows

Moziah Bridges was like any other kid when he was growing up, except for a few disadvantages. His dad wasn't around, so he was raised by a busy, single mother. They didn't have much money or possessions, but this kid had a dream to do something big.

He heard someone say, "You have to dress up to go up." Not completely sure how to do that, he looked around at people who dressed very well. Over time, he decided he really liked bow ties. So, at nine years old, he designed a bow tie that he felt looked better than ordinary ones do. He wanted to look sharp and stand out. Creating bow ties energized him, so Moziah, who goes by the nickname Mo, created a bunch of them. His grandmother was a retired seamstress and taught him how to cut and sew fabric. His mom, Tramica Morris, encouraged him to work hard and helped him start a company at age nine. He called it Mo's Bows, and soon, he had a breakthrough.

At age eleven, Moziah Bridges got to appear on the television show, Shark Tank, in 2013. On the show, one of the judges, Kevin O'Leary, made an offer to help him, but Kevin would get partial ownership of the company. Later, another judge, Daymond John (who had not made an offer) said he would mentor Mo for free, as long as he didn't give up part ownership of his company to anyone, including Kevin O'Leary.

Mo took Mr. John up on his offer. John explained later that he identified with Mo, since he was the son of a single mom and worked with her on her clothing business out of her house. Thanks to the help of his grandmother, his mother and his mentor, Daymond John, Mo has built an amazing business.

Then, another breakthrough happened in 2015.

A Big Deal

The National Basketball Association heard of Mo's Bows and decided he was a cool kid who made cool ties. They wanted to make a deal with him. They asked Mo to design a special bow tie for all thirty of their NBA teams. That year, Mo signed a seven-figure deal to license his designs and began designing the bow ties immediately. Mo's mom has taught him to budget their money, manage the sales, and they've spoken with other professional sports teams about making a bow tie for them. Mo now has several full-time employees, along with his mother, and he creates the designs in Memphis, Tennessee.

Mo is careful to express his gratitude to his grandma and his mom for all they've done for him. He is also extremely thankful for his mentor, Daymond John, for all he's done to launch his work. "He gives me great advice," Mo said. "He told me to always stay humble and always stay true to my brand. And always, most importantly, take care of my mom."

Think It Over, Talk It Over

1. What do you like best about Mo's story?
2. How do you think Mo made his decision on starting a company that makes bow ties?
3. Have you ever thought about creating a product or starting your own organization?

To watch a video about this young leader, go to: ICantWaitBook.com

I Can't Wait!

Mikaila Ulmer

Me and the Bees

Mikaila's story began when she was very young. She found out she could change her world at four years old. Her story started, however, with a little pain. She said, "When I was just four, I got stung by a bee, and then got stung again less than a week later! Naturally, I didn't enjoy bee stings at all and I became scared of bees. But then, after doing some research about them, I became fascinated and learned all about what they do for me and for our world."

Not long after this, Mikaila's family encouraged her to make a product for some competitions: The Acton Children's Business Fair and the Austin Lemonade Day. Instantly, she put on her thinking cap. As she was thinking about what to do, her great grandmother, Helen, sent her family a cookbook from the 1940s, which included her special recipe for flaxseed lemonade.

Then, Mikaila got an idea.

What if she could overcome her fear of bees by doing something with them and for them? She found out that many bees are dying, and their population is getting smaller. Mikaila decided to use her Great Granny Helen's recipe to make lemonade using the honey that bees create, instead of sugar. She later called it Me & the Bees Lemonade, and she gives part of the money she makes to help save the bees.

Her slogan is: "Buy a Bottle...Save a Bee."

Her Business Started Buzzing!
She began letting folks sample her lemonade at entrepreneurial events (for people who start companies), and people loved it. She also set up a lemonade stand right in front of her home. Slowly, her lemonade began to sell well. Today, her award-winning, ready-to-drink Me & the Bees Lemonades come in five refreshing flavors, and they are "buzzing" off the shelves of Whole Foods Market, The Fresh Market, World Market, H-E-B stores across Texas, and Kroger stores in Houston. The lemonade is also available at a growing number of restaurants, food trailers and natural food delivery companies.

Mikaila is now speaking to kids about starting a business all over the place. Her first book, Bee Fearless, Dream Like a Kid, launched in August 2020. Published by Penguin Random House, it is about her adventures in being a social entrepreneur and heading up a purpose-based brand aimed at offering great, all-natural lemonades in a way that helps save the bees.

Everyone I know who hears Mikaila's story is amazed that she not only created a product for people that tastes great, but that she used the very painful event she endured when she got stung and did something positive with it, knowing that bees will die if people don't help them. She turned a negative experience into a positive one.

Think It Over, Talk It Over

1. What surprised you most about Mikaila's story?
2. Have you ever turned a bad experience into a good one? How did you do that?
3. How could you create a product or a service that would help others?

To watch a video about this young leader, go to: ICantWaitBook.com

I Can't Wait!

Maya Penn

Creative Clothes

Maya was just eight years old when she got an idea. Her idea is now very popular, but back in 2008, she was ahead of the curve. Maya saw that very few people were doing anything about the harm they were doing to others. What harm, you ask?

As a young girl, Maya saw that sometimes the dyes and colors in clothes can hurt the person who wore them (such as through allergies). She also found out that at the time, many children were used in a harmful way to create these clothes in sweatshops. Maya believed this was wrong and that it was unnecessary. She knew people could do better than they were doing.

So, she began creating some clothes that were environmentally safe and also beautiful.

As people became interested in them, she founded a company in 2008. Maya's Ideas is an award-winning fashion brand that creates sustainable, artisan crafted accessories and clothing made from organic, recycled, and vintage materials. In starting this business, she fulfilled two dreams. She wanted to combine her two biggest passions:

- Keeping our environment safe.
- Fashion and design.

This Was Only the Beginning
Maya loves graphic design. Clothes just happened to be the first way that allowed her to sell her designs.

Since she was three years old, Maya had been drawing pictures and even began creating some animated cartoons. In fact, animation and art was always her first love. One day, when her computer got a virus, she imagined computers having a whole world inside them where creatures order technology viruses at a restaurant. It became a cartoon feature called Malicious Dishes. No doubt, Maya had an amazing imagination from the start. She created her first website at ten years old and did everything—the photos, site design, the copy, and the layout of the site's entire look.

Maya believes that being a leader is not only about building a business, but about building yourself as a person too.

Here are some of her ideas that came to life:

- Maya created a fashion brand that is sustainable and doesn't harm people or the world.
- Maya created an animated series called The Pollinators, about the importance of bees.
- Maya created a foundation to help those who are people of color to reach their dreams.

Maya Penn is a tiny, vibrant force of nature as an entrepreneur, philanthropist, fashion designer, animator, blogger, and writer. To inspire others, she even wrote a book called You Got This!

Think It Over, Talk It Over

1. What was surprising to you about Maya's story?
2. How do you think she got the idea for both creating clothes and creating cartoons?
3. What's a big lesson we can learn from Maya Penn?

To watch a video about this young leader, go to: ICantWaitBook.com

I CAN'T WAIT!

Ida Lewis

A Light for Others

When we think of superhero careers, we usually think of doctors, nurses, firefighters, or police. We usually don't think of lighthouse keepers, right? But that's what Ida Lewis was back in the nineteenth century, when she was just twelve years old. At that young age, Ida's father had been the Lime Rock Lighthouse keeper, the one who stayed in a tall lighthouse by the seashore, to keep watch over ships that might come too close to the rocks and crash against them. The lighthouse keeper would shine that light and keep boats safe as they could see the light in the darkness. Sadly, Ida's dad suffered a stroke and became disabled. He couldn't watch over the lighthouse anymore.

That's when twelve-year-old Ida became the new lighthouse keeper.

Believe it or not, Ida made her very first rescue at twelve years old, saving four men after their boat capsized in the water. A few years later, she made one of her most celebrated rescues. Two soldiers and a young guide were traveling at sea when their boat overturned. Ida, who was sick at the time, along with her brother, did not hesitate to act. She rushed to the rescue, risking her own life to save them. I'm sure Ida knew she'd be stronger and smarter if she was older—but duty called right then.

Over her lifetime, Ida Lewis saved at least eighteen lives, and was the first woman to receive the Gold Lifesaving Medal from the U.S. government. In the end, she was celebrated as the "Bravest Woman in America." Her secret? She always made the ethical choice and was a light to others in more ways than one.

She Was Different

Ida illustrates an important lesson for all of us. It is easy to see a problem that needs to be solved and jump in to solve it. Over time, however, we often forget why we got started. We lose our vision and start feeling selfish; we worry about our own comfort instead of serving others. When we forget our "why," we can stop feeling any ethical obligation to help. In short, we no longer feel responsible to do the right thing. We find it much easier to put ourselves first:

- We do the selfish thing first.
- We do the comfortable thing first.
- We do the easy thing first.

Most people are not bad people. Most human beings want to help each other and do what is right, at least most of the time. Our problem is, we begin to get lazy, comfortable, and selfish. Over time, our lives are about "us." My life is about "me." But not Ida Lewis. Even when she was past retirement age (age sixty-eight), she saved five girls who had fallen into the ocean. In short…

- She did what's right.
- She sacrificed her own comfort.
- She chose to serve others.

Think It Over, Talk It Over

1. What was it about Ida's life that makes her seem like a superhero?
2. What do you think motivated Ida to stay at that lighthouse and sacrifice for others?
3. What are some big lessons we can learn from this kid?

To watch a video about this young leader, go to: ICantWaitBook.com

If you liked the stories in

Visit icantwaitbook.com to watch videos and learn more about the stories in this book!

Appendix

Why I've Given My Life to Developing Young Leaders

It's in times like these that I am reminded of why I do what I do. I'm all about developing the next generation. Specifically, it's about equipping students to think and act like life-giving leaders, regardless of the title and position they may or may not have. I am seeing today's students step up and answer the call to lead during and after this global pandemic. College nursing majors stepped in before they earned their degree to serve in hospitals because help was needed. Liam, a junior at Yale University, took a meal to an 85-year-old woman, and it became a small movement. He recruited 1,200 volunteers to take food to shut-ins and to give them a "virtual hug."

Generation Z had already displayed a rise in activism before COVID-19 hit. Over the last few years, however, that drive has skyrocketed. Hard times often cultivate a strong generation.

For Parents and Educators

I bet you've seen this before. Often, students become interested in solving a problem; later, they identify as an activist; and eventually, they become a leader. It begins with the desire to "right a wrong" and soon becomes much bigger than merely acting as an individual. It becomes about influencing others. Thanks to social media, an act of kindness or service can multiply. So, why do students identify as activists and become leaders?

Let me offer six reasons why young people are in a perfect stage to develop as leaders.

1. Youth are developmentally ideal.
Kids ages 14–24 are mature enough to spot social injustices and energetic enough to act. During this period, people are in an ideal stage to test boundaries, question what they've assumed, and try new solutions. Everything inside them nudges them to do so. They may not be strategic, but they occupy an ideal spot to push for change. This is why many movements in history had young people at the helm. And honestly, by the time I reached sixty years old, I could see problems more clearly than ever, but was too tired to act on my observations. Young people are not.

2. Youth are neurologically perfect.
We have known for years that the adolescent brain is not fully formed. The portion that calculates the rewards for risk develops faster than the prefrontal cortex, which calculates the consequences for those risks. At first, neuroscientists concluded this merely produces risky behavior (for example, a male teen dives off a cliff because his friends are watching). However, the data shows that much of what looks like adolescent impulsivity is actually behavior that's guided by the desire to learn about the world. We now know that a teen brain is curious and attempts new ventures more rapidly than older adults do.

3. Youth are biographically available.
They're not yet encumbered by responsibilities of family and finances that would otherwise tie them down. When I was in college, I made some bold moves, attempting to reach a few audacious goals that I never would have taken on, once I was married. I was single and had no mortgage payments. I had no burdens, bills, or babies. This chapter of my story was perfect for fearless activity. I had very little to lose. Once I was married with children, I was responsible for others and had to measure my every move more carefully. In short, the recipe for boldness is often young, single, and idealistic. It's the perfect time in their story to get started.

4. Youth are informationally prepared.
In school, they learn about societal issues and want to respond beyond taking a course. One of the challenges of students today is they are overexposed to information earlier than they're ready and underexposed to firsthand experiences later than they are ready. Much of a teen's life today is artificial — exams, video games, sports, Netflix, or virtual reality. They long for genuine, high-stakes pursuits. They want to do something about what they know, not just write a paper about it. Their smartphone has exposed them to problems in our world, and they often long to instantly respond to them.

5. Youth are intellectually unfettered.
Kids are not bound by established paradigms that limit older, more experienced adults. As we age, our library of mental paradigms is set, often in concrete. Our neural pathways no longer enjoy the plasticity of our younger years. We've formed our views of the world and how it works. We frequently become more jaded and cynical. We often get stuck. We say things like, "We tried that before, and it didn't work." Teens are not bound by our paradigms and can solve problems by seeing possibilities adults no longer can see.

6. Youth are dispositionally hopeful.
I mentioned this briefly above, but when we're young, idealism and optimism begin to peak; kids believe they can create change. Studies show optimism reaches its peak in our younger years and begins to decline over time as we age. It may explain why children believe in Santa Claus and the Easter Bunny. But it also explains why kids ask questions about why certain social injustices exist or why organizations endure dysfunctions. The teenage disposition, while it can be apathetic, can also be empathetic and passionate when developed well by parents, teachers, coaches, and employers.

Consider this lesson from history. Tough times frequently cultivate a strong generation. (Just examine the kids who grew up during the Great Depression and fought in World War II.) Strong generations frequently cultivate good times. Good times often cultivate weak generations, who in turn lead to tough times. As I look at our world today—I'd say we're in tough times. Could we leverage these times to develop our kids into a strong generation of adults?

In August 2018, twenty-year-old Matt Deitsch and eighteen-year-old Emma (X) Gonzalez appeared on The Daily Show with Trevor Noah. They discussed the "Road to Change" summer tour, which they coordinated alongside the "March for Our Lives" student activists. As the interview came to a close, Trevor Noah could see that these young people were better informed about the issues and more immersed in policy than many politicians. He said to the young interviewees, "You know, you guys have the right to be kids as well, right?" Matt responded in part by saying, "I know you want us to be kids, but we have more important things to do."

Let's get them ready to do those important things.

Why Today Is the Right Time to Develop Young Leaders

When I was in high school and college, I don't remember anyone talking about leadership. It was not a topic of conversation; it was not a course I could attend; it was not even a challenge that adults (teachers or coaches) gave me on campus. It is safe to say—leadership wasn't even a category in my mind.

The first mention of it, as I remember, was at a conference I attended as a university senior. John Maxwell spoke, and he affirmed that he believed those who thought and acted like leaders were measurably more valuable to an organization.

I went to work for him the very next year.

At the time, most leadership books were books on "management" or how to organize people and tasks. Most of them didn't address the issue of vision, inspiration, emotional intelligence, or even teamwork. Fortunately, the topic has evolved. Today, there are far more resources on leadership, and I, for one, am grateful so many students and young professionals are getting involved.

If you're considering expanding what you offer in terms of leader-development (in school, at home, on an athletic team, or at work), let me incentivize you. Below are eight reasons why now is a perfect time to equip emerging leaders to serve.

1. There is more free "do it yourself" content available today than ever.
You need not look far to locate free ideas and guidance. There is endless video content out there on sites like YouTube and TED Talks. I have spent a good chunk of the past twenty years helping colleges establish leadership minors, creating a developmental process and a series of resources enabling students to grow sequentially. Even on their own, students can find tools to help them lead better.

2. The problems and needs of the world are available to see on-line.
Most students hold a portable device in their hand every day, and on that device, they can see the needs of the world vividly. When I was young, a kid had to be intentional to discover what was going on globally, regarding crises like dirty water, malnourishment, human trafficking, poverty, housing, and so on. Today, the challenges are everywhere, and students are finding them and responding to them.

3. Students don't need a "sponsor" to get started or to build a platform.
Twenty years ago, an entrepreneur, musician, artist, or author usually had to be "noticed" by a publisher or an organization to gain a platform to launch an idea. Not anymore. Amazon lets you publish your own book, iTunes lets you broadcast your own song, and GoFundMe enables you to raise money for a cause you believe in. Forget "white collar" or "blue collar" jobs. Today, we have "no collar" leaders who start to build their reach at home.

4. Teens are more open and interested in leadership than in the past.
Since leadership has come into vogue, and books on management have morphed into genuine content on leadership, today's young generation has taken notice. Adults are talking about leadership, and the need for good leaders is obvious. A 2016 Universum survey revealed that globally, Generation Z teens are more interested in leadership than either of the previous two generations. Many want to serve by leading.

5. The inspiration of others is posted every day, sparking ideas for solutions.
Thanks to social media, students can now observe how others are solving problems in communities and gain inspiration from such posts. Just like there are "copycat crimes" on school campuses, there are "copycat service projects" too. Students can interact with others who share the same passion for issues and gain ideas, receive motivation, and even troubleshoot together. This has given them momentum.

6. Leadership is now a popular subject that is gaining traction in schools.
Unlike decades ago, leadership courses are now offered in every state of the U.S. and at both high schools and universities. In 1986, approximately seventy colleges offered courses in leadership. By 2006, leadership had become a discipline with co-curricular courses nationwide. Today, over two thousand colleges offer leadership studies, including majors and minors. The subject has expanded to high schools as faculty have recognized its importance. We are privileged to be a resource to many of the best ones, including a countywide program called Gwinnett Student Leadership Team (GSLT), which invests in select sophomores through seniors in the metro-Atlanta area.

7. Our young have a keen intuition of where culture is heading.
Some fifty years ago, Margaret Mead keenly observed the future belonged to the young, who will figure out where the culture is heading faster than adults will. They can almost see the future; they perceive where history is taking us. They understand technology, trends, and ideas that will work in the future. Often, college students respectfully tell me, "I don't look to adults for cues on the future. I know what I want to start, and I don't plan on waiting for a company to launch me."

8. The need for leaders is greater than ever in modern history.
This is my opinion, but let me offer my case for it. Because we have more people on earth today than at any time in modern history, we likely have more problems too. Humans are loaded with both potential to reach and problems to solve. What we need now are ethical servant-leaders who serve by leading and who lead by serving. We are all about equipping students to solve problems and serve people.

How to Spot a Leader Early

If we're serious about developing leadership qualities in our kids, we must identify what those qualities are and define the outcomes we know to be realistic. I believe there are raw materials inside students that provide early clues to their leadership predisposition. We accelerate their progress if we can spot them early. Let me illustrate.

In 1921, young Franklin Delano Roosevelt was diagnosed with polio. It was a deadly disease until 1957. The diagnosis changed any expectations of a normal life for an adult. Polio crippled nearly everyone who contracted it. Most recognized they were destined for life in a wheelchair.

At the same time, a friend of Roosevelt's contracted polio as well. The two men drew closer to each other, having a common struggle with a shared disability. While both young men ended up in a wheelchair, their lives turned out radically different. FDR's friend took the "road most traveled." He slowly became passive about his condition. Eventually, he grew bitter, even angry at his handicap. It is easy to understand. He was never able to do the sort of things that young men do with women, sports, and their vocation. Roosevelt's friend shrunk from ever expecting anything worthwhile of himself, and eventually died an unknown and quite melancholy man.

In contrast, Roosevelt decided to make the most of his situation. You might say he took the "road less traveled." He believed in his gut he was supposed to amount to something and positively influence others. He saw his disablement as a way to identify with the marginalized in society. It gave him courage and perspective on those who suffered. After entering a career in civil service, he later went into politics. The disease actually helped him reach his goals. Franklin D. Roosevelt served as our U.S. president during the Great Depression and World War II and became the only president elected to four terms of office.

I've often asked myself how two individuals with similar circumstances could reach such different outcomes. Roosevelt's friend had every reason to grow bitter and merely survive such a hellish childhood. He was a victim of his circumstances. On the other hand, Roosevelt refused to think like a victim. FDR grew through his circumstances and became an effective leader during a most difficult period in our country's history.

Roosevelt's is not an isolated story. Other incredible leaders in history fought horrific diseases during their early years. Sir Isaac Newton, Michelangelo, and Leonardo Da Vinci all had epilepsy. Abraham Lincoln struggled with chronic depression. Thomas Edison and Ludwig van Beethoven were both deaf. Harriet Tubman was vision impaired, and Galileo went completely blind. For some reason, the struggle did not diminish them.

These leaders rose above it all.

Look for PRIDE: Five Intrinsic Signals
We see pride today in many performers, including athletes, actors, singers, you name it. I believe authentic leaders possess a different kind of pride. It constitutes a set of qualities that are early predictors of leadership in young people. Check out this list and note any you see in the students around you. Possessing even one of them can be an indicator of future leadership. If a kid has all five—you can almost rest assured that they'll be leading something in their future.

While I believe every child and young adult has influence and can learn to be a leader, I believe there are at least five intrinsic leadership signals that some kids send to their parents and teachers as early as the third and fourth grade. These five words spell the word: PRIDE. They're the same signals that FDR, Newton, and Lincoln must have sent as kids. They can be seen when children interact with both peers and adults. Check out these early leadership predictors in young people:

1. Perception
The first leadership signal youth demonstrate surrounds the way they think. They perceive the world a bit differently than most of their peers. They can see a bigger picture. While they likely remain most concerned with their own needs, their perspective extends beyond those needs. They see how situations impact others around them. They are able to fly 30,000 feet above the ground and get a bird's-eye view of those situations and respond accordingly.

This trait can show up in several ways. A ten-year-old may arrive at a restaurant with her parents, knowing they'll be meeting up with friends or extended family for a meal. Without instruction, she enters the restaurant determining how big the table must be and how many chairs they'll need to request of the hostess. That's an early signal of leadership. It begins with perspective.

2. Responsibility

This is a second signal kids send to adults that leadership qualities exist innately within them. They feel responsible for results. Even as young children, they assume they must help solve problems, or correct false statements, or even help someone who cannot do something for themselves. Often, these students pay attention to details and seem to care about elements their peers might find trivial or not worth their attention. At other times, their sense of ownership isn't displayed in detail as much as an effort to make sure the final, desired goal is reached.

The Gallup Organization created an instrument years ago called Strengths Finder. One of the 34 internal strengths that humans possess is: responsibility. Those who demonstrate responsibility are often an organization's best workers. At Growing Leaders, we seldom hire staff or interns if they don't display responsibility as one of their top five strengths. It is the natural bent to cover bases and take ownership without being told to do so.

3. Initiative

A third leadership signal young people demonstrate is initiative. This is the internal drive to act. When they perceive something could be done to improve conditions, they believe it should be done and they step out first to do it. They don't necessarily wait for peers to support them. Sometimes they don't even wait for adult approval. At times, they don't even wait to see if their behavior is the norm or is safe. They go first.

This drive can lead students to do some very stupid things—things they might get punished for—because they can't stand their current conditions. But we must remember: it is an early sign of leadership. The young person's perception is clear and their displeasure is compelling. I've known kids to get involved in recycling bottles, or raising money for a friend who has cancer, or even collecting clothes and food for Haiti because they have a strong sense of initiative.

4. Dissatisfaction
This one may be counterintuitive. An early signal in a student might be a negative emotion. Before they display talent, vision, or planning skills, you might just see discontentment residing inside them. It occurs when she spots a reality she deems wrong. It seems mediocre or unjust or evil and needs to be changed. The feeling inside the young person looks negative, not positive. It may display itself in raw emotion like anger, grief, disappointment, frustration, or sadness. We must help them transform that bad attitude into a good action.

Young Martin Luther King, Jr. couldn't sit still as he watched racial inequality during the 1950s and '60s. The injustice pushed him to speak, to march, to organize sit-ins and demonstrations and meetings and boycotts. He admitted to being angry early on, but his response was intentional, guided by his study of Mahatma Gandhi and the message of Jesus. He decided the movement must be peaceful and meaningful—impacting southern cities where it counted: in their budgets. Today, we must help students respond, not react, to negative emotions; we must help them turn discontentment into a sense of duty.

5. Energy
One more early predictor of leadership is raw energy. While I realize leadership and energy are not synonymous, very often the student who brings energy to the group is the one who ends up leading. Sometimes peers assume the one who has it is a natural leader. For instance, statistics tell us that the kid who speaks first is often expected to lead. This can show up in charisma, a sense of humor, a predisposition to talk or react, but young leaders frequently bring a positive vibe and energy to others. Most kids wait for someone else to set the cues.

While in kindergarten, Collin displayed all kinds of energy on his first day, and his teacher decided to capitalize on it. She told Collin he would be a leader for the class—and promptly channeled his energy into very clear directions for his fellow students to follow. It ended up being an incredibly positive experience that year for everyone.

After his first week, Collin told his dad that he'd been asked to be a leader. When his father asked what that meant, he got a great life lesson from his son. Collin simply said: "I get to open doors for others." What a simple summary of what leaders for others—they open doors for them.

Even if it's moving in a wrong direction, an early indicator of leadership is vitality and drive inside a young person. They exude passion that is contagious with others.

My Takeaway
I believe there are two obvious action steps I can take as an adult who wishes to build leadership qualities in students. First, I can look for these intrinsic qualities in students and position them in authentic leadership roles. Second, I can nurture these qualities in my own kids and in the students around me. These qualities (perception, responsibility, and initiative) are life skills we must not fail to develop in our future leaders. The qualities are not difficult to see. Students who possess them will demonstrate problem-solving skills as they encounter challenges. They will be a source of solutions. In short, they will:

- See it. (Perception)
- Own it. (Responsibility)
- Act on it. (Initiative)

FOR DISCUSSION . . .

1. Have you seen these five qualities in any non-positioned student?
2. Do you believe there are other essential predictors of leadership potential?
3. How could you incorporate and identify these qualities as you observe your kids?

About the Author

Dr. Tim Elmore is the founder of Growing Leaders (www.GrowingLeaders.com), an Atlanta-based non-profit organization created to develop emerging leaders. Since founding Growing Leaders in 2003, Elmore has spoken to over 500,000 leaders in businesses, universities, athletic teams and non-profit organizations, including The Home Depot, Coca-Cola Bottling Company Consolidated, American Eagle, Ford Motor Co. and Chick-fil-A as well as the San Francisco Giants, Tampa Bay Buccaneers, Ohio State University, Stanford University and the University of Alabama athletics department.

His work grew out of twenty years serving alongside Dr. John C. Maxwell where he focused on leadership for the emerging generations. Elmore has appeared in The Wall Street Journal, the Washington Post, USA Today, and Psychology Today and he's been featured on CNN's Headline News and Fox and Friends to talk about leading multiple generations in the marketplace. Tim was listed in the top 100 leadership speakers in America by Inc. magazine. He has written more than 35 books, including the best-selling Habitudes: Images That Form Leadership Habits and Attitudes. His latest book, A New Kind of Diversity: Making the Different Generations on Your Team a Competitive Advantage released in the fall of 2022. Tim and his wife, Pam, have two adult children, Bethany and Jonathan. He and Pam live outside of Atlanta. You can also find his work at: TimElmore.com.